With a Highland Regiment in Mesopotamia

General Sir Stanley Maude and His Staff, Baghdad, 1917

With a Highland Regiment in Mesopotamia

The 2nd Battalion, The Black Watch in Iraq during the First World War, 1916-1917

H. John Blampied

LEONAUR

*With a Highland
Regiment in
Mesopotamia*
The 2nd Battalion, The Black Watch in Iraq
during the First World War, 1916-1917
by H. John Blampied

First published under the title
*With a Highland
Regiment in
Mesopotamia
1916-1917*

Leonaur is an imprint
of Oakpast Ltd

ISBN: 978-0-85706-122-5 (hardcover)
ISBN: 978-0-85706-121-8 (softcover)

http://www.leonaur.com

Contents

To the Children of the Officers and Men
of *The Black Watch* Regiment
Briefly Describing the Doings
of the 2nd Battalion in Mesopotamia
Written so That They May Not Forget
the Hardships Endured and the Sacrifices
Which Have Been Made
on Their Behalf 1916-1917.

———

Author's Note

In writing this short account of the 2nd Battalion, *The Black Watch,* in Mesopotamia, my aim has not been to write a military history of all that was achieved; that will be the task of some one more competent to judge of merits and demerits than myself. My object has been to give an account in simple language of the two years spent by the Battalion in the Iraq, so that the children of the men of the regiment may know of the brave deeds and the hardships cheerfully borne on their behalf.

Two articles describing our last two battles are here reprinted with the permission of Brigadier-General A. G. Wauchope, from whom I have also received many details of our earlier fights, and I am also indebted for information to Captains J. Macqueen, W. E. Blair, W. A. Young, Sergeant-Major W. S. Clark, and other officers of the Battalion.

Mesopotamia, October, 1917.

Telegram from His Majesty the King.

Received by Colonel A. G. Wauchope, D.S.O., Commanding, 2nd Battalion, *The Black Watch,* January 1917.

I thank you, Officers, Non-Commissioned Officers and men, for the card of New Year's greetings.

I have followed the work of the Battalion with great interest. I know how well all ranks have done, what they have suffered, and that they will ever maintain the glorious tradition of the Regiment.

George, R.I.,
Colonel-in-Chief.

Order by G. O. C., 7th (Meerut) Division.

I cannot speak too highly of the splendid gallantry of *The Black*

Watch Highlanders, aided by a party of the *6th Jats*, in storming the Turkish Trenches.

Their noble achievement is one of the highest.

They showed qualities of endurance and courage under circumstances so adverse, as to be almost phenomenal.

> Sir George Younghusband,
> Commanding *7th (Meerut)* Division.

After the action fought on the 21st January 1916 on the Tigris the above was published.

Letter to O. C. 2nd Battalion, The Black Watch.

Tell the men of your battalion that they have given, in the advance to the relief of Kut, brilliant examples of cool courage, and hard and determined fighting which could not be surpassed.

> Sir Percy Lake,
> Commanding the Army in Mesopotamia.

July, 1916.

General Munro, C.-in-C, Indian Army, addressing The Black Watch Regiment, Tigris Front—October 1916.

Your reputation is well known, I need say nothing more.

To The Black Watch Regiment.

From Sir Stanley Maude, Army Commander—March 1917.

You led the way into Baghdad, and to lead and be first is the proper place for your Regiment.

LEONAUR EDITORS' NOTE

When this book was first published, during the First World War, the name of the regiment - The Black Watch - was withheld, together with the identity of the Author. The present publishers have taken the liberty of revealing these, together with other originally omitted information, for the modern reader. These entries are shown in Italics.

CHAPTER 1

Bound for Mesopotamia

At the outbreak of war, the 2nd Battalion *The Black Watch* was stationed at Bareilly, having been in India since the end of the South African War. Of the fighting in that campaign, the 2nd Battalion had had its full share. At first it formed part of General Wauchope's Highland Brigade and fought with traditional stubbornness at Magersfontein and Paadeburg, and later on identified its name with many of the captures and some of the hardest marches of that campaign.

On the mobilisation of the Indian Corps, the 2nd Battalion formed part of a Brigade of the *7th (Meerut)* Division and landed in France early in October 1914, and were in the trenches holding part of the line near Festubert before the end of the month. At no time, except in the early months of 1916 in Mesopotamia, was the battalion so severely tried as in these first two months in France. The conditions certainly were comfortable neither to mind or body. The trenches were knee deep in mud and water, and were without dugouts or shelters; the enemy were in great numbers and combined their aggressive tactics with the use of trench mortars and grenades, weapons of which we had neither knowledge nor training; of rest for man or officer there was little, yet no yard of trench entrusted to the battalion was ever lost either in France or Mesopotamia.

With the spring came better times, and at Neuve Chappelle a fine victory was won at small cost, but on the 9th of May the battalion suffered heavily in making an attack from the Orchard in front of the Rue-de-Bois. Often and with pleasure have we in the Iraq looked back on that summer spent in Picardy. Scouts and snipers, machine gunners and bombers, we all have different memories of those stirring days as the battalion moved from month to month along the trenches from Givenchy Hill to Northward of Laventie; and of the days of rest in billets behind Bethune, Richebourg and the Rue de Paradis; memories of close comradeship, of well-loved friends, of most noble deeds and of lives freely given for King and Country. But the day we recall now and shall ever recall as the red letter day of the year is the 21st of September. Five battalions of the regiment joined that day in the battle of Loos, and though separated in the line, at one in spirit, all five battalions swept forward regardless of loss, driving the enemy from their trenches, captured line after line of the position and penetrated deep into the German defences.

The 2nd and 4th Battalions had attacked together from Fauguissart and, in reaching the Moulin de Pictre, an advance of two miles made with little support on either left flank or right, the losses had been so severe that the two battalions were afterwards amalgamated into one under the command of Colonel Wauchope. These two battalions, in conjunction with another Highland Regiment under Colonel Thompson, despite several attacks and four mines being blown up within our first line, held Givenchy Hill throughout October. Then, when the Germans quieted down in this neighbourhood, we returned to our old line near the Rue de Bois.

There rumour had it that the Indian Corps was soon to be sent to Mesopotamia. Some welcomed the idea of change, no one looked forward to another four months of the mud of Flanders. Almost everyone who did not know imagined that they would be giving up every discomfort which the winter brought for a picnic in the East, and a quick, successful and enjoyable march to Baghdad, and so when the rumours were confirmed, the whole battalion was in great spirits. Some obtained short leave to say 'Good-Bye' to their friends across the channel before leaving for the East, where there would be no short visits home, no getting letters and parcels daily, but the Regiment had gained great honour beneath foreign skies, so probably it was going to add to them even if it was only establishing marching records along the Tigris to their goal at Baghdad. Besides, was not Townshend and his gallant force in danger in Kut? And the idea of forming part of the relieving column appealed to every man.

So at the end of November the regiment entrained behind that long Western Front where they had fought for so many months against such terrific odds, and where so many gallant comrades lay buried, and everyone was happy, and no one thought that within a few short weeks the battalion would practically cease to exist. Before they arrived in France, many had never left the shores of Great Britain, and now they were embarking on an expedition that would reveal to them some of the wonders of the East. Is it any wonder, under those circumstances, that no one was downhearted?

The train journey through the heart of France from the mud of the trenches, leaving the cold and cheerless days behind for the sunny south was full of interest, and of looking forward to what was in store. Marseilles, that busy Mediterranean Port which has seen such wonderful scenes of troops arriving from all parts of the world, and of all colours, naturally turned out to see the regiment it had welcomed to defend its Frontiers a year before, and which was now *en-route* to defend and fight for the honour of the Allied cause three thousand miles away. And so on December the 6th, it was 'Good-Bye' to the pleasant land of France, and the regiment embarked on the Transport nine hundred and fifty strong. Having suffered heavy casualties on the Western Front, few of the original number left France, bound for Basrah *via* the Suez Canal.

Before leaving, in appreciation of the stubborn fighting in the battle of Loos by the 2nd Battalion, the Cross of the Legion of Honour was conferred on the commanding officer, Colonel A. G. Wauchope, D.S.O. Never was an honour more richly deserved, never was the conferring of one more popular. No one who has not served in the regiment can possibly be aware of what the colonel has done to make his battalion one of the most efficient in Mesopotamia. I was very interested in listening to a story told me by a brother officer who was standing alone in a traverse of a trench. Two staff officers were talking in the next traverse and he heard one remark: "Of course, out here at the present the regiment is Wauchope, and Wauchope is the regiment." It is a name most closely connected with the fortunes of the *Black Watch* Regiment.

The journey was a pleasant one; the wonderful change from the damp depressing dugout to a comfortable cabin was appreciated by the officers, and a dry and comfortable place to sleep in, instead of trying to sleep in the mud of a fire trench was welcomed by the men.

The usual stay at Port Said after successfully evading the submarines, where the wily Arab fleeces the unsuspecting Tommy, was not without interest. The *Padre* tells an interesting story about how, when he was returning from home leave to the regiment in India in 1913, he had his fortune told by one of the many fantastic liars that fatten on the stories they weave in this Eastern cesspool. The Fortune-teller told him that within a year he would be returning to Europe by the

At the Base. Scene on a creek below Basrah.

COLONEL A. G. WAUCHOPE, C.M.G., D.S.O.,
COMMANDING THE 2ND BATTALION THE BLACK WATCH.

same canal. In those piping days of peace he never suspected that it would be with the regiment on Active Service but when almost to the day and within the year, he passed through Port Said on his way to France, this one saying at least of the Fortune-teller was forcibly brought home to his mind.

Egypt in December is delightful, and more than one expressed the wish that for a time at all events they could be stationed in this most wonderful country. The Canal displayed enormous activity, there had been no such activity since the days when it was made. Thousands of Arabs and others toiled and died in making this great work. Today the Canal is guarded by thousands of troops. Enormous camps have been established at different places, and Posts are in existence all along the waterway. It being so narrow, 3-worded conversations take place between the troops on the banks and the men on the Trooper. 'Who are you?' asked the men on the bank. When the reply is returned, shouts of 'Good Old Scotland' are raised ashore. Some asked, 'Where are you going!'

'Mesop' they say.

'Poor Devils', is the encouraging reply. Then some lonely soul asks if any of his Regiment are on board, and so it goes on all day. Some swim out from the shore and shout and talk, but one is chiefly impressed by the great number of men guarding this important waterway.

At Suez a short stay is made. The water is a wonderful opal colour; the great desert on our left, the barren rocks, sunburnt and bare on our right, help to make a fascinating picture. One remembers the first time one had passed through the Canal, years before in time of peace, and how one had been filled with admiration for the medical officer who came out to the Mail Boat to give it a clean bill of health to pass through the Canal, because she was a woman, and standing month after month of Suez summer weather, which proves too much for many men, leave alone women.

But the stay is short and so as the sun sets, making wonderful colouring over the desert and sea, the journey down the Red Sea is commenced. The Red Sea in December is shorn of its terrors and can be quite enjoyable. Aden is passed, two or three days steaming along the inhospitable coast of Southern Arabia and the entrance of the Persian Gulf is reached. The Straits of Ormuz have the reputation of being one of the hottest places on earth. The rocky, and wild Arabian coast looks very beautiful in the sunshine with its innumerable islands, and

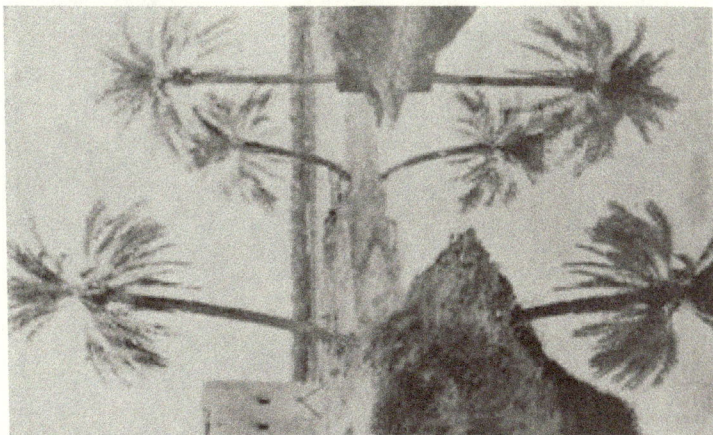

SCENES ON THE CREEKS BELOW BASRAH.

G. J. Anderson. H. W. Bruce, Capt. A. M. Grieve,
S. F. G. Alexander, D. H. Anderson.

C. J. McConaghy, Capt. A. M. Grieve, S. F. G. Alexander,
H. W. Bruce.

Chapter 2

The River

It takes about seven hours from the mouth of the river to Basrah. The journey up is of interest as none have been here before, and everything is new. Both sides of the river the banks are covered with palm trees, stretching inland for distances varying from 500 yards to three miles, and after that all is desert. We pass Abadan on our right where the pipes of the oil fields belonging to the Anglo-Persian Oil Coy. reach the river from Ahwaz. It has been said that the Mesopotamian Campaign was started in the first place to protect these oil-fields. One wonders now if it would have been advisable to protect them and hold Basrah only, and not push forward further inland. But it is easy to be wise after the event, and high politics, tactics and strategy do not form part of an account of the doings of the 2nd Battalion—so I must not be led astray.

The river is very broad and is navigable for hundreds of miles. Mohammerah, the Persian town at the junction of the Shatt-el-Arab and Karun rivers, looked an interesting place. It is; as many months later I was fortunate enough to be able to spend some time there. The Sheikh of Mohammerah has proved a good friend to the British, and almost opposite his palace one can see the remains of the three steamers in the river which the Turks sunk in a vain endeavour to block the passage as they retreated; as good fortune or Providence would have it, one boat in sinking swung round and left the passage open. At Mohammerah is a big Convalescent Hospital for white as well as Indian troops.

We noticed some large barrack looking houses on our left, one in particular, 'Beit Naama', attracting attention; but more about that later on as this establishment has now been turned into an hospital for officers. And so at last anchor is dropped off Basrah, as 'Ashar' is usually referred to as 'Basrah' by everyone out of the actual place. Was this the romantic spot from which Sinbad the Sailor started on his wonderful voyages?—was this the spot that so many have imagined must be one of the wonderful places of the East?—when they are thousands of miles away from it. A famous traveller has said, "that its European inhabitants only remain alive during the day through a perception of the humour of their situation, and by night through the agency of the prayers of their despairing relatives." For Basrah has the most malarial air, the most choleraic water, and the most infernal climate of any spot in the world outside 'Tophet.'

One company of the regiment had travelled out on a different transport—with another Highland unit and arrived a day or so in advance and were awaiting the arrival of the main body at Basrah. They were very interested in the place and were full of their adventures and of rumours. One thing was evident, one thing alone mattered, troops were needed, urgently needed, at the front; and we were at once ordered to proceed up river. The regiment transshipped in midstream, not even having time to land, and were taken up by two river boats, with barges attached on either side.

Not a man who made that journey and is still alive will ever forget the "P-7" or the *Salimi*. The time since leaving France had not been wasted; everything that could possibly be done to keep the men fit and their minds active was done. Physical drill every morning, sports were got up, concerts,—the colonel himself taking a big interest and share in everything that tended to the comfort of his men. At the best of times, life on a Troopship is a cramped existence, but in comparison to the up river voyages, it is a life of luxury. The world has been scoured for river boats for this campaign; steamers from the Nile, the Irrawady and the Thames are doing excellent work in carrying troops and supplies to the fighting line.

Part of the river is so narrow that it is dangerous for paddle boats to attempt the journey without lighters attached as bumping into the sides of the bank the paddle boxes would be smashed. The trip up the river in January is by no means a pleasure one. It is not now! and it was much less so in January 1916. The nights are cold and in the early morning the river is lost in mist. At nights it is usually necessary to tie up at the side of the bank or to anchor in midstream. Only on bright moonlight nights, and not always then, can progress be made. The flood season on the Tigris is at its height about May and continues so till about the end of June. The river gradually falls in July and August

The *Padre*

THE QUARTER-MASTER

Everyday Scenes In Ashar.

Ashar Barracks

STREET SCENES IN ASHAR.

and is at its lowest level during the months of September, October and November. It rises during the rains in December and January, sometimes as much as four or five feet, and this keeps the river fairly high during the following two months. In April the river rises still higher owing to the melting of the snow on the mountains in the north. These are the normal changes that come as regularly as winter follows autumn. There may be slight variations such as more rain one winter season than another, for instance, January 1916 was far wetter than January 1917. There are occasional high floods owing to the rain, and in January 1896 the river rose eight feet in one night at Baghdad.

The men crowded on to the barges attached to the side of the paddle boats and of course everything was of interest, everything was new in this, the oldest country in the world. Because Kurnah at the junction of the Tigris and the Euphrates has the reputation of being the site of the Garden of Eden, many and various are the jokes which have been made against this most unfortunate of places by members of the Expeditionary Force, but all amount to the one thing—that Adam and Eve had very little to lose in being driven out, if it is unchanged since those days.

The belt of Palm trees which so attracted our attention along the banks from the mouth of the Gulf to Basrah still continues, but they are thinning down very considerably and by the time Kurnah is reached the belt has no depth at all. There is no question of a halt, no question of a rest, "Push On" is the order of the day. It may seem somewhat absurd now, but it brings home to one the eagerness of all to share in the relief of Kut, that the first thing the colonel did on landing at Basra was to wire to the corps commander at the front asking him to arrange for the battalion to follow up the Relieving Column if it had passed Ali Garbi before the regiment arrived. Regardless of risk, regardless of orders, urged on by the colonel, the two steamers bearing the battalion pushed forward by night as by day for fear of not overtaking the relieving column. The winding of the river seemed interminable to those eager to be at the front, and there is little to relieve the monotony of the flat plain, save the colouring at dawn and dusk, and the appearance of a few *mahelas* floating down stream with their broad sails outspread to catch the north-west wind.

At Kurnah the Palm belt ceases and only at odd places and around villages are trees again to be seen. One cannot fail to be struck with the enormous possibilities the country offers for cultivation if only properly irrigated. Thousands and thousands of acres of the best of

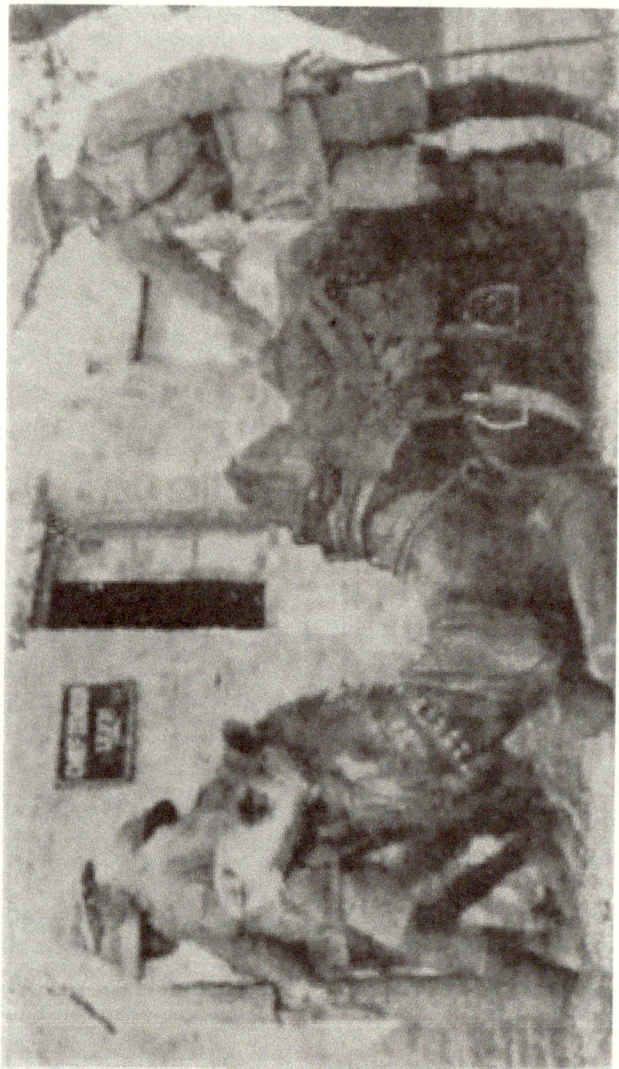

Capt. MacQueen, R.A.M.C., On His Way to Europe

Entrance to Ashar Barracks

Basrah Barracks.

Arabs Enjoy an *Al Fresco* Meal of Dates.

The Sheik of Zobeir and His Son.

Arab Bazaar.

soil, and everywhere as flat as Salisbury Plain.

We now begin to see small Arab villages along the banks of the river; they look dirty and dilapidated. The Arabs look filthy, but some have very pleasant faces, and both men and women impress one with their strength. This campaign is of course not only an eye-opener to them but also a God-send. They beg and steal on every possible occasion and on going through the narrows a lot of amusement is obtained in bargaining with them. The troops crowd on to the barges, as they bump along the sides of the river banks which are only two or three feet higher than the barge, and buy from the Arab women and children running along the banks selling eggs and fowls; as the demand has risen the prices have also advanced, and whereas at the opening of the campaign one could buy a dozen eggs for four-pence, by January 1917, I have seen officers pay two-pence each or more.

It is scarcely safe to jump ashore, as any moment the boat may launch out again into the middle of the stream, but when tied up by the bank waiting for another boat to pass brisk business can be carried on. The boats going up usually give way to those coming down, as the ones coming down may have wounded and sick, and all must be done to get them down to hospital as soon as possible, and so the time passes. At one end of the Narrows is Ezra's Tomb, a building surmounted by a blue tiled dome, which is evidently of no very ancient origin. We were informed that the edifice had been erected in memory of Ezra by a wealthy Jew, and that the place had become a sort of place of pilgrimage. Clustering round it is a small Arab hamlet with the usual sprinkling of Palm trees, and an abundance of dirt and filth, without which surely the Arab could not exist.

At the northern end of the Narrows is the village of Qalat Sahib with its minarets and lovely reflections. Then, Amara is sighted. We are now one hundred and twenty miles from our base and this place makes a kind of a half-way house between Basrah and Baghdad, and for the first time the battalion lands in Mesopotamia. It was about three o'clock in the afternoon that the order to disembark was received. Wonder was expressed at the command as everyone knew that this was still a long way behind the firing line, and was it the intention to march the rest of the distance, and if so, why? as we were so much needed.

All these queries and doubts however were soon put an end to when it became known that the colonel had decided to land and practice an attack. He knew that at any moment his regiment might

33

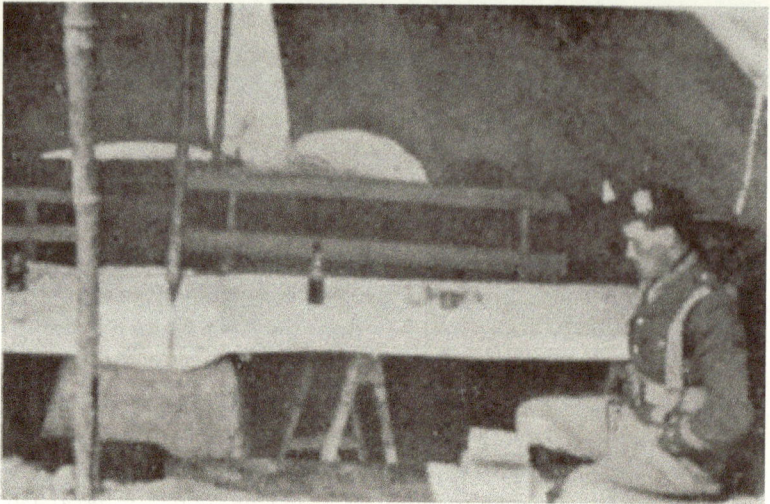

THE OFFICERS MESS, FALAHIYAH,
THE ADJUTANT, CAPTAIN N. M. RITCHIE, D.S.O.,
STUDIES MILITARY LAW.

J. M. COWIE, T. HENDERSON, A. A. YOUNG (KILLED), G. V. STEWART,
T. GILLESPIE (KILLED).

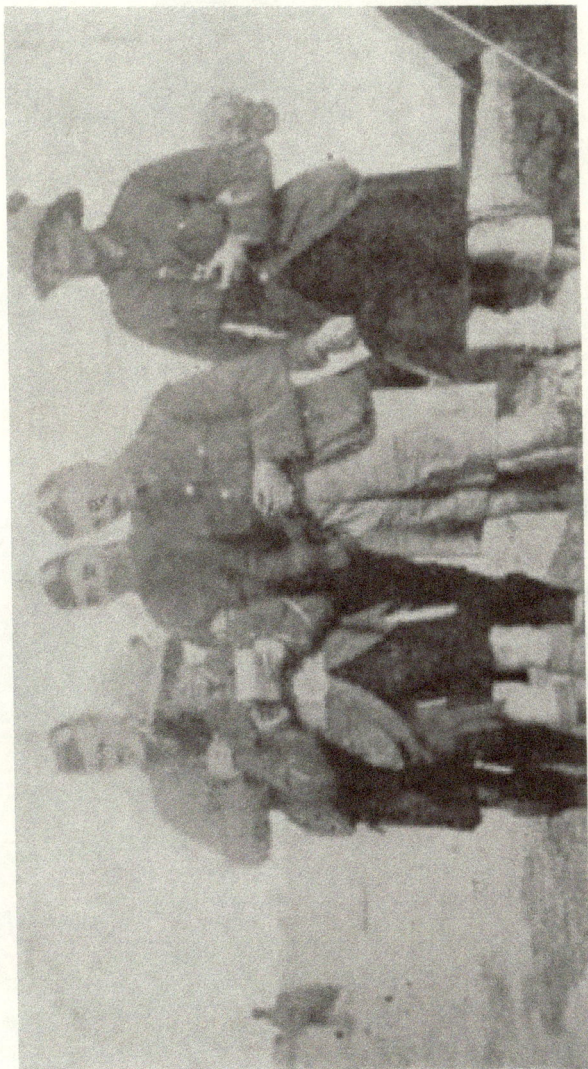

J. M. Cowie, G. V. Stewart, T. Henderson, J. H. Cotterell (Killed), H. W. Bruce (Killed).

At The Bar.

River Scenes

be thrown into action, and as the long journey was found to have a stiffening effect on one's limbs he decided on some small practice manoeuvres before the actual and real thing took place.

What a pleasure to get on shore again! At such a moment a regiment is almost like a boy's school let out after hours; everyone was in high fettle and pleased, our long journey was nearing its end, and very soon we would be relieving General Townshend who had been locked up in Kut since December 5th.

By three o'clock all were ashore and an attack on an imaginary enemy was practised, and of course victory achieved; but on returning to the river, it was found that the boats had moved up a mile or so, and tired and weary the Regiment had to go in search of them, and to add to the discomfort the rain started to come down, so that by the time everyone was on board again at seven-thirty it was dark and the men were wet, and a very subdued regiment ate their evening meal in comparison to the high spirits of earlier in the afternoon. However, very soon it would be goodbye to the boats for good, as it was expected that the following day we should land at Ali-el-Gharbi.

CHAPTER 3

Near Annihalation

The 2nd Battalion disembarked at Ali-el-Gharbi, one hundred and eighty miles from Basrah. The ground was little better than a bog from the rain of the previous day; with very little rain the whole country-side seems to become a quagmire. The mud is about the most slippery kind to be found anywhere, so that walking is made most difficult. The first work was to unload the barges. All the kit, supplies, and tents had to be taken ashore as we were leaving the boats for good and were now in a hostile country. The unloading is a tedious business and one of the most tiring of fatigues, but when the whole of a regiment is put on to it the work is soon finished. That night No. 1 Company was on Out-Post duty and the rest slumbered.

The following morning broke fine and sunny, as so often happens in this country after wet and miserable evenings. The clouds roll up during the night and the morning is such that one feels it is good to be alive. There was a sharpness in the air that made it almost impossi-ble to think that in a few months' time this country would be proving itself to be the hottest in the world. The orders were to be up at dawn and start immediately after breakfast. Part of the Brigade transport was of camels, but the camels getting out of hand disappeared into the desert and the start had to be made without them.

It is a fascinating picture to see a long line of camels in single file starting off on a voyage across the desert. But this misadventure had delayed matters and the heat after midday was very trying for march-ing although in the distance one could see the snow on the higher summits of the Pusht-i-kuh Mountains which form the dividing line between Persia and Turkey. From an aeroplane the picture of the Ti-gris flowing through this flat country with all its numerous twists and turns must resemble a huge snake. A short halt was made in the middle of the day for lunch, and a final halt was not called till within five miles of Sheikh-Saad, and a distance of twenty-two miles had been covered, not bad work, considering the regiment had just landed after being cooped up for a month on transports and river boats.

But everyone was dead tired and exhausted and No. 1 Company was pleased that they had provided the out-Posts the previous night, and that it was the turn of No. 2 to do duty. General Younghusband with part of his division had moved out and engaged the enemy, and that night we could see the flashes of the guns and hear the constant rattle of musketry. At break of day General Aylmer, the corps commander, rode out past us to the advanced force, but it was not till after nine o'clock that our brigade advanced some five miles and lay down to await orders. The orders were clear and promised success.

One brigade was to deal with the Turks on the right bank of the Tigris, one brigade was to hold his forces near the left bank, while a third, with ours in immediate support, was to make the decisive attack on the enemy's left flank. This brigade and ours therefore manoeuvred to the right for position. Before we had taken sufficient ground to our right, fresh orders arrived directing both brigades to counter-march back and attack the centre of the enemy's line, against which the brigade on our left was already moving. Instant action was demanded and instantly the 2nd Battalion and a battalion of *Jats* moved forward to the attack. No time was given for the issue of orders, no frontage or direction was given, no signal communication was arranged.

To all enquiries the one answer was given "Advance where the bullets are thickest" and right there did the 2nd Battalion advance. Magazines were charged and bayonets fixed on the move; the companies moved with great rapidity and wonderful exactness considering the exhausting march of the day before and the little practice they had had in open warfare. But without covering fire, and there was little artillery fire available to cover our attack such an attack over bare open plain cannot succeed unless the enemy be few in numbers or of poor heart. The Turk was neither weak nor faint-hearted, and poured in so deadly a fire that before the leading lines were within 200 yards of the enemy, five hundred of the battalion had been killed or wounded.

Other units suffered with almost equal severity, the attack came to an inevitable halt, there were no reserves to drive it home, consequently orders were sent up from the Brigade that the infantry should dig themselves in where they were. Nineteen officers and two-thirds of the men had been hit: Colonel Wauchope was severely wounded by a shell and Major Hamilton Johnstone took over command.

But if our losses were heavy and the sufferings great, the Turk had also suffered so heavily at our hands, that he was forced to evacuate his position on the following day, and we occupied it on the 9th. The situation was one of extreme difficulty for the new Commanding officer. If there were few men left there were still fewer officers or sergeants remaining with much experience. Yet the Turks were close to our trenches and re-organisation of the depleted platoons imperative. But his indomitable spirit and the determination within the regiment, so often shown at times of crisis, made the hardest tasks possible. The wounded were brought back, the dead buried; rations were got forward and the trenches securely held. New leaders were appointed, and on January 10th when the Brigade moved forward from Sheikh-Saad the Battalion had been reformed under its well-loved commander, ready as always to do whatever duty lay before.

Progress was made up the river bank slowly, but always in the direction of Kut, the aim and object of our every march and fight at this period. The enemy had retreated some miles and, on January 13th, they were attacked and driven out of their position on the *wadi*, the 2nd Battalion playing a small but successful part in this action and losing 34 men. The Turks then fell back on to a more strongly entrenched position at Hannah.

The rainy season was now in full swing. It rained day after day and the whole country became sodden, making it very difficult to move troops and almost impossible to move artillery. The discomfort the men suffered is almost indescribable, with no tents and everyone chronically wet to the skin and unable to have properly cooked food, made a seemingly hopeless position; but it is wonderful how hardship and discomforts are forgotten at the thought of beleaguered comrades in need of help and, as the country dried up and the sun shone forth, the men's spirits rose.

On the eighteenth the 2nd Battalion had orders again to move forward. They did so and occupied a line of trenches about two thousand yards off the enemy, who were strongly entrenched in what is now known as the Hannah position. The whole country here, it must be understood, is absolutely flat, only in the distance twenty or thirty miles away one could see the snow-clad Pusht-i-kuh Mountains. Each night short advances were made and fresh trenches dug, till the night of the 20th. In this manner an advance was made up to within two hundred and fifty yards of the enemy's position. There, under cover

THE PIPE BAND.

CORPORAL McLEOD

Our Left Flank At San-i-yat, The Tigris.

At Mohammerah

CAPT. HALDANE INSPECTS THE HANNAH TRENCHES

of darkness the last line of trenches were dug and the companies deployed into two lines, and there they faced the enemy and awaited dawn. The Battalion and our old friends, the *Jats*, had been lent to another Brigade detailed to make the decisive assault on the morning of the 21st.

Major Hamilton Johnston had made every possible arrangement for a successful assault and the leading lines were well within striking distance of the enemy. But however brilliantly carried out an assault may be, however gallant and determined the men, to ensure a lasting success against a determined foe there must be weight as well as depth in the attack. Now on the night of the 20th, owing to the movement among the troops, lack of reconnaissance and the mud, the troops in rear of the two leading battalions were deployed so far back, that though they moved forward in the morning simultaneously with the *Jats* and Highlanders, they suffered such losses on their way that none were able to reach the enemy trenches. And dire was our need there for support.

At a given signal our artillery opened a light bombardment of seven minutes, then the long awaited and thrilling order to assault was given. The companies made a magnificent response and all rushed forward, crossed the muddy water-logged No Man's Land with their left 200 or 300 yards from the river, and gained the objective, though not without losses. No pause had been made for firing for the bayonet was the weapon our men trusted. More and more it is proved that the bayonet is the weapon that wins the trench, the rifle the defensive weapon that holds it. Yet though no pause had been made our losses in that charge were severe. Major Hamilton Johnston was struck first by bullet and then, almost at once, killed by shell; only four officers reached the objective and of these three were wounded.

The Turks fought desperately and it was only after a severe struggle that we captured some 300 yards of the first line trench. The *Jats* had suffered fully as severely as ourselves, but a certain number joined up with our men and fought right well, but no further assistance was forthcoming. The colonel was once asked by the Higher Command if such and such a trench could be captured. "My Regiment," he replies, "will capture any trench, but it is a different matter whether it is possible to hold it." Then for one and a quarter hours, the length of time which the trench was held, the regiment added a very glorious page to its history.

Great gallantry was displayed and Lieutenant M. M. Thorburn who was severely wounded by a bayonet thrust received the Military Cross as an immediate award. The enemy counter-attacked from two sides and our few bombs, though replenished from some captured from the enemy, were soon expended; but many charges up the trenches were made to bomb them out, two machine guns were captured and put out of action.

Slowly however the Turks drove the remnants of our platoons towards the river and the killed and wounded greatly outnumbered the survivors, 2nd Lieutenant Souther was wounded but refused to retire, and every moment the situation was getting more desperate. 2nd Lieutenant Henderson assumed command and was gallantly supported by C.S.M. Proudfoot and Sergeant McDonald. Seeing that the position was untenable, C.S.M. Proudfoot asked 2nd Lieutenant Henderson if he did not think it would be wise to fall back as no assistance was being sent, and men were being uselessly sacrificed. "How can I order the Regiment to retire?" he replied. C.S.M. Proudfoot and Sergeant MacDonald were both killed. Two of the finest men in the regiment they were, and both had been recommended for commissions.

Proudfoot would have made a splendid officer; he had perhaps the finest physique of any man in the Battalion and for long had been the best reel dancer. No one who ever knew Sergeant MacDonald will forget him. His soft voice and gentle manner, his readiness to help whoever had need endeared him to all, and many a brave deed had he done as scout leader of the Battalion both in France and Mesopotamia. It now became impossible to remain unsupported in the enemy's position. Slowly and in good order some eighty men, one quarter of those who had started the attack two hours before, retired across No Man's Land and regained our trenches.

When muster roll was called ninety-nine men remained of this gallant Regiment, out of the nine hundred and fifty who had landed in Mesopotamia less than three weeks before. As many wounded as possible were brought in. The *Padre*, Major the Revd. Macfarlane did splendid service. Darkness was closing in as the Regiment fell back on to the second line, and the very skies wept at the tragedy being enacted below them. No tents, no warmth, all soaked to the skin, intense cold, and defeated. It is possible to be happy even if wet, cold and hungry if you are victorious, but to be wet, cold and defeated, and yet undaunted is worthy of the highest traditions of heroes.

The following day what remained of the Battalion was moved across the river, and 2nd Lieutenant Stewart Smith assumed com-

Captured Turkish Officers.

Turkish Prisoners Arrive At Basrah.

mand, to be followed shortly by Captain Crake.

The stay on the right bank of the river was short, and the remnants of the Battalion were again soon on the left bank, but the losses of the Highland units engaged had been so heavy that it was decided to form one battalion of what remained, under Colonel Thompson. This brilliant officer was shortly afterwards given a brigade, and during the Campaign of the winter 1916-17 did such excellent work that he was rewarded with the command of a division again proving that age should not be regarded as a deterrent for promotion if ability is conspicuous. He was only forty when commanding a brigade. During February and March the battalion suffered great discomfort, not to speak of hardships. The rainfall was unusually heavy and the country all mud. Difficulty was experienced in getting up supplies. And every day and every hour the Turks were tightening their hold on Kut, so gallantly defended by General Townshend and his brave division. For in reading the history of the battles of this spring, we must always remember that the relief of Kut was the object in view, and for that object our Generals were right in giving battle and in accepting any odds while one chance remained of final success.

The regiment was now encamped near the Hannah position, fresh drafts arrived, re-organisation completed and training continued in bombing, trench digging and minor manoeuvres. The great effort on the right bank of March 8th had failed, but within a month another supreme effort was made on the left bank. Another Division had arrived from Gallipoli and, on April 5th, under General Maude, their trusted commander, this Division captured the Hannah position. On the evening of the same day, they gained the Falahiyah trenches and on the same night our column, with the Highland Battalion leading, marched through Falahiyah and advanced up the edge of the Suwakie Marsh with the intention of attacking the Turkish left.

As so often happens, however, on a night march, some delay occurred, and at dawn the troops had not reached their objective and were not fully deployed. The Turks opened a very heavy fire practically destroying our leading platoons and, as we were still some six hundred yards from their trenches, the order was given to dig in where we were. This was done, but the weather this year was beyond all precedent, the marsh kept on rising and before evening it had flooded our men out of the new trenches. We were consequently ordered to retire three hundred yards and dig in afresh.

On the 7th a demonstration in force was carried out by fresh troops;

J. F. C. DIXON, M.C

S. L. HUNTER

A. B. CUMMING (KILLED 22-4-16).

ZOBEIR MINARET.

little was effected by this demonstration as it was checked mainly by shell and machine gun fire before advancing very far. Like many another effort of these heart breaking days, it was fore-doomed to fail; and the spirits of the troops and their fighting value was only maintained by the stern resolve that every man would continue fighting, no matter against what odds, so long as the flag was still flying over Kut.

On the night of the 8th, another division took over our trenches, and on the following evening made a night advance and attacked the San-i-yat position. Heavy casualties were incurred, but they failed to reach the enemy's position. We therefore again took over and held the trenches until April 22nd. A final attack was planned for that day to be made by two Brigades, but at the last moment the Brigade on our right found the ground in their front impassable owing to the rising of the marsh. Consequently in the assault we were exposed to a heavy fire from our right flank as well as from the front. Nevertheless the gallant Highlanders swept across the muddy ground, drove the enemy from his first line and assaulted the second. Lieutenant Forester led his platoon against the third line, but from that gallant assault none returned. Major Inglis, the senior officer with the Battalion, and many another were killed. The enemy trenches were in most places filled with water, to consolidate our position was impossible and, fired on from three sides, the survivors of the Brigade were forced slowly back to their original position. With new drafts the Highland Battalion had attacked at full strength, but suffered during the day over 600 casualties.

The position now in Kut was almost hopeless, and General Townshend began to destroy his stores and guns. One last but very gallant attempt was to be made to get supplies in, and the General Officer Commanding the Expeditionary Force reported as follows:—

At 8 p.m., on April 24th, 1916, with a crew from the Royal Navy under Lieutenant Firman, R.N., assisted by Lieutenant-Commander Cowley, R.N.V.R., the *Julnar*, carrying 270 tons of supplies left Falahiyah in an attempt to reach Kut. Her departure was covered by all Artillery and Machine gun fire that could be brought to bear, in the hope of attracting the enemy's attention. She was, however, discovered and shelled on her passage up the river. At 1 a.m., on the 25th, General Townshend reported that she had not yet arrived, and that at midnight a burst of heavy firing had been heard at Magasis, some 8½ miles

VIEWS OF BEIT NAMA HOSPITAL.

IN THE GARDEN OF BEIT NAMA HOSPITAL

THE HOSPITAL LAUNCH

A HOSPITAL SHIP.

OFFICERS' TENTS, FALAHIYAH.

THE MESS TENTS, FALAHIYAH.

THE REGIMENT MOVES OFF.

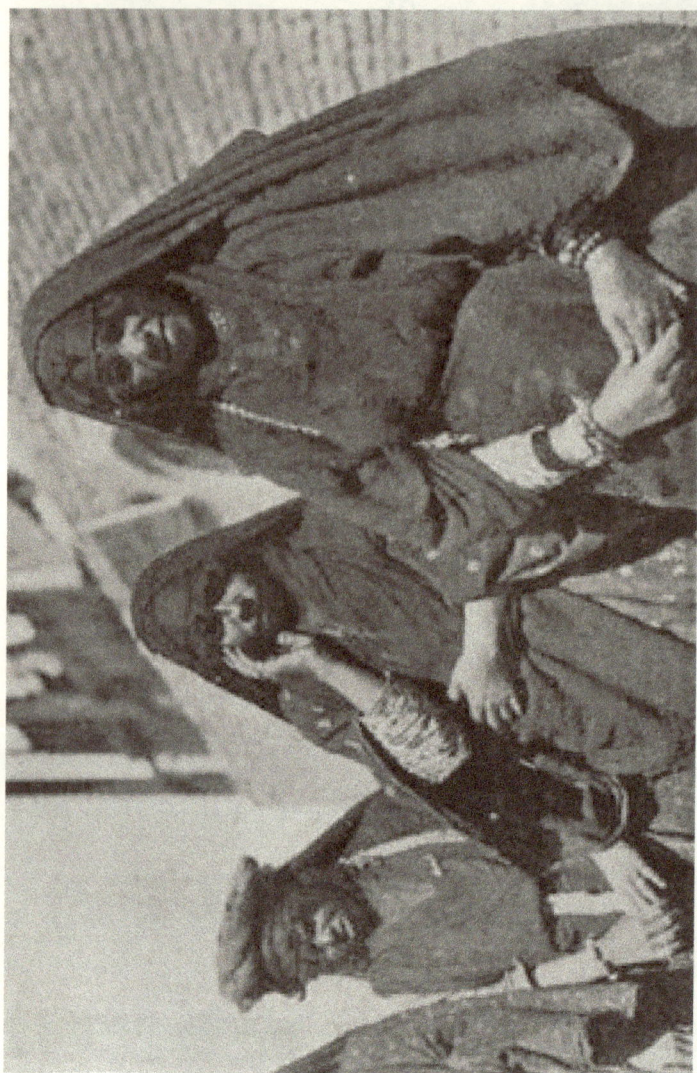

ARAB GIRLS.

from Kut by river, which had suddenly ceased.

There could be little doubt that the enterprise had failed, and the next day the Air Service reported the *Julnar* in the hands of the Turks at Magasis. The leaders of this brave attempt, Lieutenant H. O. B. Firman, R.N., and his assistant Lieut.-Commander C. H. Cowley, R.N.V.R., the latter of whom throughout the campaign in Mesopotamia performed magnificent service in command of the *Mejidieh*, have been reported by the Turks to have been killed, the remainder of the gallant crew, including five wounded, are prisoners of war. Knowing well the chances against them all the gallant officers and men who manned the *Julnar* for the occasion were volunteers. I trust the services in this connection of Lieut. H. O. B. Firman, R.N., and Lieutenant-Commander C. H. Cowley, R.N.V.R., his assistant, both of whom were unfortunately killed, may be recognized by the posthumous grant of some suitable honour.

ADMIRALTY.

The King has been graciously pleased to approve of the posthumous grant of the Victoria Cross to the undermentioned officers in recognition of their conspicuous gallantry in an attempt to reprovision the Force besieged in Kut-el-Amarah:—

Lieut. Humphry Osbaldeston Brooke Firman, R.N.
Lieut.-Comdr. Charles Henry Cowley, R.N.V.R."

After a stubborn defence for one hundred and forty-three days, General Townshend's supplies were exhausted, and he was compelled to surrender on April 29th, with 9,000 men.

On the Banks of the Tigris. 125° in the Shade.

Beit Nama Hospital.

A Winter Sunrise. Beit Nama Hospital.

ONE OF THE NOBLE BAND OF SISTERS.

CHAPTER 4

Consolidation

The strategical importance of Kut-el-Amarah lies in the fact that it is at the junction of the Shatt-el-Hai with the Tigris. The force which controls Kut has the choice of movement down the Hai or the Tigris at will, and this advantage was with the Turk.

The summer was rapidly advancing with its awful heat and the enemy, unable to press his advantage any further, was quite willing to remain in his trenches and await events. And so for seven months both sides resorted to trench warfare, and sat down facing each other through the most trying period of the year.

The Secretary of State made the following announcement: "General Lake reports on May 20th that the right (South) bank of the Tigris is clear of the enemy as far as the Shatt-el-Hai, except for small rear-guards covering the bridge over the Hai some 500 yards below its junction with the Tigris. Our main force on this bank has reached the line Magasis-Dujailah. On the left (North) bank the enemy are reported to be still occupying the San-i-yat position. Weather is intensely hot and trying, and temperature during the last few days has been over 100 degrees in the shade."

Owing to the melting of the snows in Asia Minor the Tigris is at its highest in the spring and early summer and the left of our lines stretched to the water edge. The Suwakie marsh is also very full at this season and forms a natural protection to the right flank of the San-i-yat position. Consequently as the front held was under two miles the lines could be safely held by one brigade at a time, with the other two in reserve. The procedure adopted during the summer months was for one brigade to hold the trenches, one brigade in the forward area rest camp, and the other the rearward area rest camp, situated at the Bridgehead opposite Arab Village, some six miles behind the firing line.

Fresh troops were arriving in the country daily, drafts to different regiments to make up for those killed, wounded and sick. A great number coming direct from England and Scotland and quite unaccustomed to the great heat went sick immediately on arrival in the country.

In addition, however, many wounded were now returning, the numbers at the front increased, and in May, Colonel Thompson was appointed to the command of a brigade on the right bank, and Colonel Wauchope took over the Highland Battalion. Throughout the summer our division held the San-i-yat position. In spite of numerous drafts the Highland Battalion remained considerably under strength both in men and officers until August. By that time the battalion was about twelve hundred strong, and it was split up into its two original units, our comrades being posted to another brigade.

These two battalions had served together as the Highland Battalion during a period of their history that will never be forgotten. Close friends in India, the two battalions had now fought shoulder to shoulder in many a hard-fought action, they had captured and defended trenches together under conditions sometimes so desperate that only their faith and confidence in each other enabled the two regiments not only to maintain their glorious traditions but also to enhance their reputation. No jealousy marred the good feeling between officers and men; there was nothing but goodwill.

We all had absolute trust in Colonel Thompson, and Colonel Wauchope has often said he always found the same spirit, the same wholehearted readiness to perform every duty equally amongst both units. In some ways the platoon, in some ways the division is the tactical unit of the British Army, but by tradition, custom and wholesome practise the living organism is the battalion, and the commander who ignores that fact loses a source of strength that no other factor fills. It was only the strength of fellowship and their confidence in their two commanders that enabled these two famous regiments to work and fight under every adverse circumstance so wholeheartedly and with the single-minded devotion which they always showed during these trying times.

The bond of sentiment holds when other bonds fail. To all to whom regimental feeling appeals there is no sight like the swing of the kilt, no sound like the sound of the pipes. Men of both regiments might often recall how they had charged forward in France, the pipers

Guns And Boat Captured From The Turks.

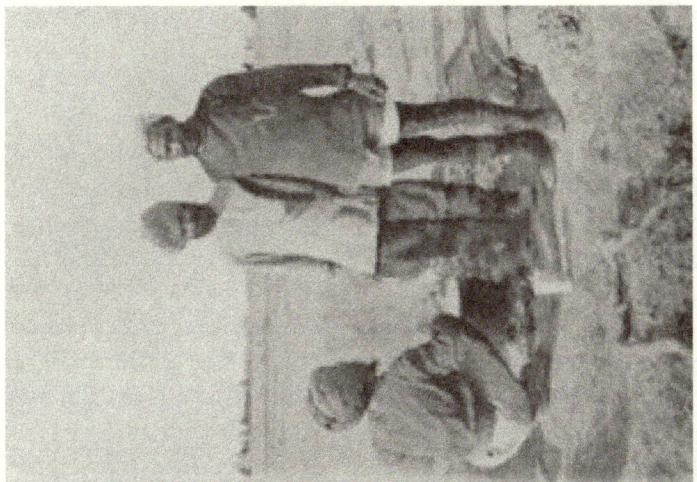

TYPES IN MESOPOTAMIA.

leading the way, and no body of men had themselves shewn greater gallantry or inspired others with their spirit more than the regimental pipers.

Yet even in war the days of battle are few and the days of trial many, and many a time at reveillé and retreat, on the march and in camp has the sound of the massed pipers stirred our memories and stoutened our hearts to face whatever danger or hardship lay before. The old Crimean *reveillé* was still heard, but a new *reveillé*, "The Highland Regiment in Mesopotamia," arranged by Pipe-Major Keith, was played more often. During a long march "Scotland's my Ain Hame," and "Neil Gow's Farewell to Whiskey" were often call for, and, on reaching camp, before striking up with "The Blue Bonnets," the pipers always played the colonel's favourite air, "After the Battle."

In these days lack of tents, and the excessive heat were minor troubles compared to the prevalence of sickness and constant flow of casualties. Whatever the strength of the battalion, the duties had to be performed. Again and again men left their turn of sentry duty only to take part in one of the innumerable but essential working parties. Over and over again men had to work throughout the cooler hours of the twenty-four, and pick up what rest they might in the heat and glare, amid the dust and flies, of midday. But if there was much sickness there was no grumbling, and the energy and thoroughness with which all duties were performed will remain for all time a lasting credit to the men of the regiment.

The average age of the company commanders was one and twenty, yet the C. O. told me that never was a colonel better served in this and every respect. The adjutant was under twenty, but no more capable or devoted officer was ever adjutant to the regiment. The sergeant major was absent sick, and during part of the time there were but four sergeants remaining with the battalion; but the young men specially selected to fill the vacancies, responded to the call, accepted all their responsibilities, and never was the standard of discipline or smartness higher in the battalion. Of the many awards given to the battalion I doubt if any were better deserved than the D.S.O. gained by the adjutant, and the two Military Crosses awarded in succession to our two regimental sergeant-majors. To these might well be added the four D.C.Ms. gained by the four sergeant-bombers, two of whom added a bar to their medals, and unsurpassed by any, the D.C.M., with the bar, gained by the stretcher-bearer sergeant.

On August 28th, General Maude took over command and his

wonderful capacity for administration was soon manifested. Also more boats were arriving for river transport, more supplies, both Medical and Military, were being sent out. Control of the campaign was taken over by the War Office. Canteens were established at different points, enabling both officers and men to buy small luxuries, and the Y.M.C.A. had branches established at many places. The country will never be able to thank the Y.M.C.A. enough for what they did for its soldiers in Mesopotamia.

The hospitals were being rapidly well established, and excellent work was being done to provide all necessary accommodation and comfort for sick men and wounded. Casualty Clearing Stations were in full swing, and hundreds of men were sent down the line from hospital to hospital, in many cases to eventually be sent to India in an endeavour to be restored to health after having endured all sorts of privations and hardships in Mesopotamia. An excellent Officers' Hospital was established at Amara, and went under the name of the "Rawal-Pindi Hospital." It was well run and had a large and capable staff. There were other hospitals at Amara for officers and men and improvements were being added daily.

There was a large number of hospitals in Basrah and a very fine one called the Beit Naama Hospital about six miles below Basrah, beautifully situated on the banks of the river and surrounded by palm trees, was opened in June 1916 to try and relieve the pressure of officers coming down river, which No. 3 British General Hospital could not easily cope with. This place was fitted up with electric light and electric fans, hot and cold water baths, lift, ice and soda water factories, up-to-date "X" Ray installation and an operating theatre for surgical cases.

They took in on an average about 135 officers a month and sent on an average 28 to India. It had accommodation for 100 officers and had a staff of three medical officers, a matron and seven sisters. The work done by the nursing sisters in this country, the untiring devotion to duty displayed under most trying climatic conditions when the temperature rose to nearly 130 degrees in the shade, is beyond all praise, and only those who have seen and suffered in this campaign should be competent to judge.

THE SECOND IN COMMAND

The Doctor in the Trenches

Amongst the Palm Trees

CHAPTER 5

Trenches

All these improvements, all these reinforcements, all these extra supplies could have but one meaning and but one end in view, and that was as soon as the summer heat was over in the words of Nelson's famous signal to "engage the enemy more closely."

The time spent out of the trenches was no holiday, one talked of going back to the Rest Camp. But Rest Camp was only a kindly term; it did not mean, as one might be led to believe, a delightful camp where comfortable chairs and well-served meals were supplied to tired and war-worn officers and men. No such thing; in fact so much the opposite was the case that one often heard it remarked that one got far more rest in the trenches than in any Rest Camp at the immediate front. The colonel of the regiment was a thruster. He never wasted a moment himself and would have his regiment the same. On the great Bronze Gong of one of our battalions is engraved "I mark the hours, Do you?" Certainly the colonel of the 2nd Battalion did.

It was too hot for any drill or outside parades between the hours of 9 a.m. and 5 p.m., so everyone gasped for air inside their tents during those awful hours when the temperature rose to 124° in the shade, and the one thing one prayed for was the hastening of sunset; but if the officers or men slept or tried to sleep during those trying hours it was not so with the colonel, at almost any time one visited his tent it was to find him busy; he did not seem to know what it was to suffer from fatigue, and during all those trying summer months, when with one solitary exception every officer was off duty ill for some period of time, however short, the commanding officer was only confined to his tent for half a day. Duties commenced soon after sunrise and very often before, every opportunity being taken to make as much use of the coolest and light hours of the 24.

A very strict course of intensive training was gone through and the results were to make themselves manifest early the next year. Bombing was practiced morning and night. Bayonet fighting was excelled in, and attacks by bombers and bayonetmen were practiced with frequency in trenches especially prepared for the purpose. Officers were trained to march by compass and stars and some were even given a course of riding lessons, nothing being left to chance. The long hot trying summer was not wasted; it was a preparation for what was to come. Long marches were out of the question, but short night marches were often practiced, sometimes by the battalion alone, sometimes by the whole brigade with an attack at dawn.

These manoeuvres were very popular with everyone; it was possible to enjoy moving about in the cool of the night and the quietness and silence with which it was possible for a whole regiment to advance on to a supposed enemy position often impressed one. Having marched to a certain point from which an attack was to be delivered, the pre-arranged signal having been given, the bagpipes would burst forth into music and with a wild cheer the whole regiment would charge forward in wave after wave and the supposed enemy driven from their stronghold. A few moments' rest would be given and the C.O. would call his officers around him and explain, praise or condemn various things which had struck him and, as the sun rose over the Pusht-i-Kuh hills, we would march back to camp.

A keen rivalry and competition was established among the various platoons as to which would mount the best guard, and a very searching examination was conducted each evening by the adjutant and sergeant-major. This led to great interest being taken by the whole battalion in the mounting of the guard, and the smartness of the guard increased by leaps and bounds. The heat, of course, found its victims and in spite of all precautions there was a fair amount of sickness during the summer; it was impossible to avoid it. Great care was taken to see that all drinking water was properly chlorinated, and special waterproof tanks were erected on the river banks. If anyone went sick they were almost immediately sent to the Field Hospital where they got every possible attention. All through the summer the battalion was very much below strength and the work fell heavily on those remaining.

It was decided to hold "Highland Sports" on Wednesday, August 30th, and a number of other units, both British and Indian, were asked to take part. A suitable piece of ground was chosen some five miles

VIEWS IN ZOBEIR. THE SITE OF ANCIENT BASRAH, THE HOME OF SINBAD THE SAILOR.

THE PRESIDENT, REGIMENTAL INSTITUTES.

Captain T. W. Stewart.

behind the firing line, and on the day a great concourse of people assembled. The corps commander honoured the regiment and several generals from other brigades were also present, our own brigadier being an interested spectator. The events were keenly contested and the honours were fairly evenly divided. We won the Highland Dancing with a very fine exhibition.

Another Highland unit carried off the board jump with a record leap. The officers "Donkey Fight", a scrap "Five aside" between our officers and those of another Highland unit caused huge delight and amusement and before many moments blood was flowing freely. The mile race by the Indian Regiments drew a big crowd and a large number of entries and a great race was won by the Punjabis. The inter-company cross country run was a keen contest. 13 men were chosen from each company, with one officer in charge and an N. C. O. They had to run in full kit and packs also carrying rifles and a severe course of training was gone through. P. P. B. Miller Stirling commanded one company, the brothers Smythe (South Africans and both keen sportsmen) each commanded other companies.

I forget who commanded the fourth company. The average time was under ten minutes over a two-mile course, and the remarkable thing showing the uniformity of training was that there was scarcely two minutes' difference in time between any company. But the event of the day was the 'tug-of-war' between the two Highland Regiments. It was the best tug-of-war that many of us had ever witnessed. The sides had been carefully picked and well trained. Officers and men cheered on their respective regiments, the crowd of onlookers swelled till the whole brigade was looking on in feverish suspense, and so even were the sides that for nearly five minutes not an inch of ground was lost or gained.

The cheering ceased and the silence became intense; one could see the veins standing out on the competitors' foreheads and perspiration pouring off their faces, each man pulling to the last ounce, then our coach shouted "come away" and as if by magic they gave a convulsive pull and gained a foot, the spell was broken, and the men of our regiment looking on gave a wild cheer. In a second everyone was shouting for their side, but slowly, very slowly, inch by inch they were winning, they would lose a foot and then gain two, till after one of the sternest pulls in the history of the regiment, our opponents crossed the line and we were victors. Both sides sank exhausted to the ground as their regiments cheered them to the echo.

Perhaps some daring Turkish flying man heard that brave cheer from his observation car far above and thought the mad English were practising some new game to worry his existence. That evening at a concert given by the regiment the general made a speech and congratulated the two teams on the best tug-of war he had ever seen, congratulating them on their splendid staying powers and for the tenacity and determination they had displayed, which he remarked augured ill for the Turk in the coming months. History records how true was his prophesy.

Our brigadier was General Charles Norie whose gallantry in the field was well-known, as in some strange way gallantry ever is known, to every man who served under him. And well loved was Charles Norie. He had lost an arm fighting on the Indian frontier. There have been many depressing optimists since August 1914 who every Autumn swear the war will end next spring, and every spring know it cannot last beyond next autumn. An answer given by one of our sergeants was consonant to the serene spirit and resolution that filled the regiment and bid defiance to the future. Glancing at the general waving his one arm in the air, he answered some faint-hearted hopeful, "I'm thinking the war will not be over till Norie claps his hands." It is in that spirit that the armies of England win their way through at whatever cost.

That evening the colonel gave a dinner party and the powers of the Mess President were taxed to the utmost limit. Nearly 40 sat down, the mess staff rose to the occasion, and the cook turned out things we had never seen before. The next day the commanding officer remarked at dinner "Really, P.M.C., I don't at all know why when we have two or three generals to dinner you can give us nice white table cloths but at other times it is only bare boards",

"Well Sir," he hesitatingly replied, "they were two of Stewart's sheets."

Sundays were usually fairly slack days. I sometimes thought that they could have been even slacker, it being so absolutely necessary to have one day's rest a week. Church Parade would be held in the early morning, and another service at 6 in the evening after the sun had set. These evening services were very impressive; we would form round in a half circle sitting on the grass, or what formed a substitute for grass, with the *Padre* in the middle. The commanding officer would sit at one end of the half circle either amongst his officers or at the other end amongst the men, and the *Padre* knowing well the limits of

The P. M. C.

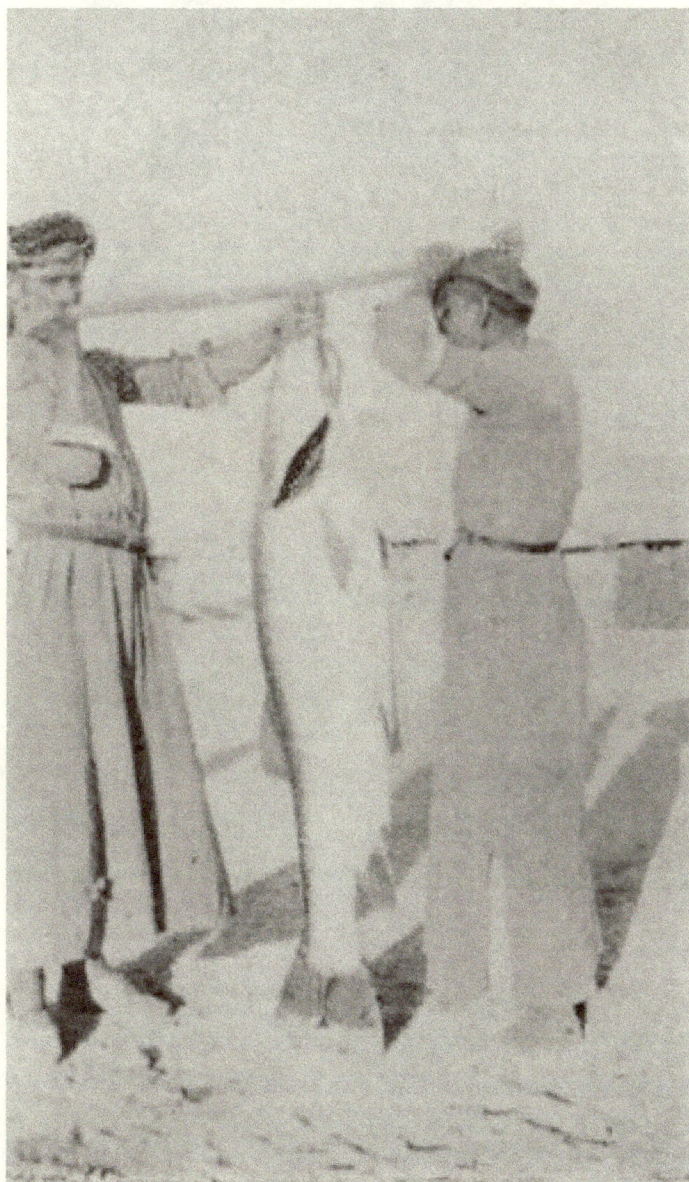

Tigris Salmon.

THE PALM CREEKS.

human endurance and the severe test that the great heat was putting us to, never preached too long a sermon. We all loved him, and as he had been with the regiment for a dozen years he knew everyone and about everyone, and when he went sick after the great advance on Baghdad, all felt that they had temporarily lost a friend.

We were miles away from any village and still further from any town, so there was no one to visit on Sundays and no social life; unlike our comrades in France we were unable to enjoy the hospitality of a friendly population or look forward to going home on leave. We were out here and we knew it meant for months or may be years. Leave in a restricted form was granted to India during the 1916 summer, but that is going from one hot country to another and, though appreciated, could not be compared to going home. We knew two or three days in advance, the day that we would go up to the trenches for our spell, and we usually went in at the commencement of the month, so had the advantage, or disadvantage as it sometimes proved, of having a full moon.

The distance to march was about three miles before we reached the end of the communication trench and we never started till late in the afternoon. All that day we were busy preparing our trench kits and packing up the necessary kit which had to be as little as possible. We always marched up in kilts and marched out in kilts, but during our stay there our clothes were the irreducible minimum, shorts and shirts. I well remember my first spell in the trenches of the famous Sanniyat position. We usually held the centre of the line with an Indian Regiment on either side and one in reserve. We left camp soon after seven, the night was one of those wonderful clear still moonlight nights for which this country is justly famous. It was difficult to imagine before one came within sound of rifle fire that a grim struggle was being enacted a mile or so in front, everything was still quiet and peaceful, there were no villages to pass through on our way up, it was simply open flat country with a river on one side and a marsh on the other, a long dusty road leading from the Rest Camps to the rear of the trenches.

A light was burning in Brigade Headquarters and a sentry on duty and we silently filed up the long communication trench which was deep in dust as rain had not fallen for months. We passed fatigue parties coming down for rations and the dust was most distressing. The relief of trenches is usually a long and tedious process—handing over stores, getting receipts, pointing out anything of exceptional interest and generally getting settled down for ten or fourteen days. The Regimental Headquarters were about 200 yards behind the front line and connected up by telephone and various companies and platoons took it in turn to do their round of duty in the front line. I think in the trenches you come to know men as you can get to know them in no other place, the reserve of civilization is often thrown off and you know a man for what he is, not for what he would have you think he is.

I remember sitting one night on the fire step of the front line trench and having a long and interesting talk with a Sergeant about Nigeria. He was telling me all about his life out there before the war, and the part he took in the Cameroon Campaign. Back in a Rest Camp he would never have got so communicative, but when one knows that one's lives are dependant on each other a close comradeship often results between both officers and men. This gallant fellow some months later was killed as his company was advancing to attack a Turkish position after the capture of Baghdad. I always feel glad I had that talk with him.

The nights in the trenches were the busiest time not only on account of darkness but also on account of coolness. At 9 o'clock in the morning an inspection of rifles and kit would be held by the company officers, after which the whole company would retire to dugouts in the reserve front line trenches, ten yards behind the fire trench and then endeavour to get through the day as well as possible. The dugouts had not the comforts of present day dugouts on the Western Front. The only roof we had was sail cloth, so if a shell happened to strike it the results were fatal. This sail cloth kept the sun off, but the heat was terrific. Sentries only, and one officer per company were kept on duty during the day in the front line, where there was not a yard of shade, the sun beat down with relentless vigour and gradually as the day wore on the temperature would rise to 120 degrees in the shade and 160 degrees in the sun and there was no shade.

And this was not for a day or two days but week after week. After 9 o'clock in the morning a death-like stillness would creep over everything, both sides suffering too much to be able to add any more suffering to each other. The stillness would be broken now and again by the crack of a sniper's rifle and one dare not look over the parapet. In the early mornings aeroplanes would fly over the lines but without any great show of activity on either side; the heat kept everything quiet. The very flies are scarce in the hottest months, only the sandflies

Ashar Creek.

Native Bazaar, Ashar.

Scenes In Basrah.

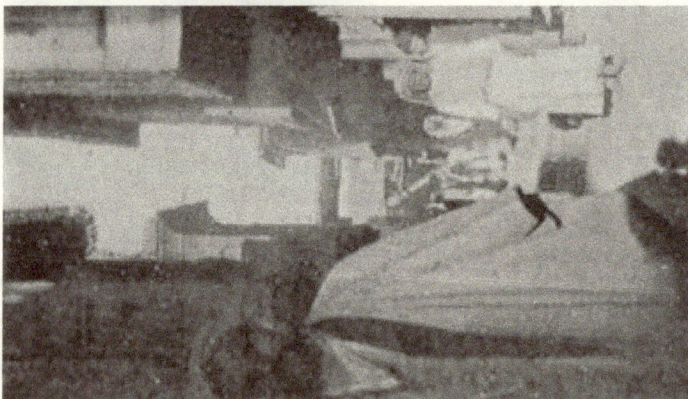

torment one at night, and so the day gradually passes, and as one goes the round to see everything is in order and one sees the men stretched out in their dug-outs, reading, trying to sleep, very few talking and all suffering, one remembers with what irritation one had read in a famous London daily paper, a query—why the Mesopotamian Campaign had come to an end during the summer, why no advance was heard of.

One longed to put the writer of that article over the parapet in the sun where within five minutes or less, he would have his question answered. At times, on a hot parching day lying in one's dugout, one would hear a great flutter of wings as a flight of cranes or wild geese flew over our lines, immediately followed by a loud fusillade of rifle fire as the sentries endeavoured to bring one down; several times a goose was brought down, and I well remember the annoyance of an officer when a goose he had winged managed to flutter across into the Turkish lines. The heat was at the maximum between 2 and 3 when we could almost boil oil in the sun.

At 4 o'clock things livened up somewhat and at 5-30 everyone stood ready in the front line awaiting any possible attack but neither side showed any intention of attacking. Night duties were arranged, parapets had to be mended, new trenches dug, barbed wire put out and all the necessary work in connection with trench warfare continued. Officers patrols were regularly sent out into "No Man's Land" to examine the enemy's wire and find out if he were sapping forward. As the summer advanced the marsh receded on the left of the enemy's line, and this gave our scouts an opportunity to patrol and harass the Turks by penetrating in rear of their left flank.

Much gallant work was done in this direction and much credit gained by the regiment, for the colonel considered that a good test of the fighting energy of a company was the vigour of its patrol duties, and a good number of the Turkish sentries, I feel sure, agreed with him. The usual night "Hate" started about six when both sides opened fire, rifle and machine gun, on the opposite trenches, this was kept up all night, some nights would be more lively than others, some nights would be comparatively quiet, but now and again an artillery bombardment would take place, when we always seemed to give more than we got. Both we and the Turk were very free with rifle grenades, but what troubled us most was a special pattern of trench mortar that threw a heavy bomb over quarter of a mile. One night I remember one landed in and blew up the whole of the regimental cookhouse;

luckily the cooks were sleeping elsewhere and it was only the dixies that suffered.

I have always considered myself a very light sleeper, but one evening I had cause to come to another conclusion. I had just come off duty from the front line and was speaking to a brother officer outside my dug-out about 9 o'clock when suddenly we opened artillery fire on the Turkish position with considerable vigour, and they replied but in a milder form. I retired and lay down in my dug-out listening to the shells whistling above and praying to Providence that none would land on my sail cloth roof. In about half an hour the bombardment ceased and one wondered what damage had been done and how many lives lost. I then slept. At breakfast the next morning remarking on the bombardment I was asked "which"?

"Which?" I replied, "why last night's of course,"

"Yes, but the first or second?"

"Well, I only heard one," I said.

"Oh! another took place at midnight," I was informed. I had slept through it and had not heard a sound. So trench life must tire one out somewhat to enable one to sleep so soundly as to be unaware of a bombardment. On still nights when possible the very perfection of the night made men less inclined to fire rifles at each other's trenches. I used to hear a Turk singing. He had a deep rich voice and I often stood in the front line or in a communication trench listening to him as his voice carried across "No Man's Land" from the Turkish line 120 yards away. It used to fascinate me quite a lot and one felt that under the eastern sky, in the land of Sinbad the Sailor and Omar Khayyam that war had not quite killed romance.

I wonder what happened to that singer. I wonder if in the great push to Baghdad and beyond he was killed or if he is now singing to his fellow-prisoners in captivity in India, or if he is still cheering on his comrades in the front line further up the Tigris. I don't suppose one will ever know, but if he should ever read these lines I would like him to know he not only cheered his own side but gave pleasure to at least one of his enemies.

We used to have three Officers' Messes when in the trenches. The Headquarters Mess presided over by the colonel and two Company Messes, presided over by their respective company commanders. The Headquarters Mess was a very comfortable affair, a big dugout, and made in such a way that ground formed the table in the middle and seats all around, the sides were well banked up with sand bags and out-

THE TREE OF KNOWLEDGE, KURNAH. SUPPOSED SITE
OF THE GARDEN OF EDEN.

ASHAR CREEK.

RUINS OF "OLD BASSORAH."

THE SHIP OF THE DESERT
PLAYS AN IMPORTANT PART IN MESOPOTAMIA.

side a small ante room where one could sit and smoke in the evening, and the roof was the sky and a very wonderful sky during those long rainless cloudless months. Round about the Headquarters, the colonel, the adjutant, the doctor, the sergeant-major, had their dugouts, and the mess did for orderly room also. The Company Messes were not so elaborate, and were situated nearer the front line and close to our own dugouts.

We endeavoured however to make ourselves as comfortable as possible, but for some reason or other the flies took a great liking to our Mess (No. 1 Company), and at any time day or night they were assembled in their hundreds on our canvas roof. We had a large war map fixed up on to the mud wall to enable us to follow events and we had occasional visits from the *Padre* and the Doctor, but it was not a healthy place, no part of the second line was; the second line was about a 100 yards behind the first, and for some reason it seemed to give the Turks much more pleasure to put their shells nearer to the second line than the first. I have picked small flowers growing on the front line parapet, but I have never seen any on the second.

During my first spell in the trenches after being in the front line, I was put in charge of the reserves in the reserve trenches and spent three awful days and four awful nights in this position. The heat seemed to be worse here than anywhere. I had to spend my days in a small 40 lbs. tent lying on the ground gasping for air as the sun poured down with relentless fury. It was burning hot from the moment it rose till it set 14 hours after over the Arabian Desert. The men were slightly more fortunate in that they had a bigger tent, but they suffered also and it was at these times that one could not but admire the spirit of the 'British Soldier.' One seldom heard a complaint, of course they were "fed up" with the heat, everyone was the Archangel Gabriel would have been, but there was never any thought given to anything else but to "stick it at whatever cost."

The officer in reserve was attached to the Headquarters Mess and so one was likely to get any news going. Lying in my tent reading, I now forget the name of the book, but I came across the passage which I will always remember "The writing which Nebuchadnezar saw on the wall."

As I read that I felt convinced that Nebuchadnezar never saw any writing on the wall and when I reached the Mess that evening, the first one to come in was the Doctor and being a good Presbyterian I felt sure he would have this knowledge at his fingers' ends, so I asked him who saw the writing on the wall and he immediately replied "Nebuchadnezar".

"Not at all," I said, and I told him I had just read the same thing in a book but felt convinced it was wrong, he felt certain the book was right.

"Very well," I said, "I'll bet you, you are wrong," he accepted the bet. The adjutant came in soon after and supported the Doctor. I now saw a veritable gold mine before me and he too was willing to back his knowledge against mine. We decided to refer the matter to the colonel, so when he came in we asked his opinion. The colonel was not only a gallant soldier but he was a cautious Scotchman.

"Well," he said, "I think it was Nebuchadnezar, but I would not be willing to back too much on it."

It is only necessary to turn to the 5th Chapter of *Daniel* to see who won the bets. That night sanction came for several N.C.O.'s and men to go on leave to India for a month. Sanction had been hanging fire for some time and the lucky ones were beginning to despair. My sergeant was among the lucky ones and I knew how pleased he would be when I got back and told him to report to Headquarters at 5 the next morning for leave to India. It was late when I got back, but little did he mind being disturbed to receive such news. I vouch for it that he slept well that night and did not oversleep himself in the morning.

To those in France who get leave every three or four months it is impossible to understand what leave even to India once in one or two years means, but when the news comes that we can get leave for England, it will indeed be a red letter day for us all. I was so exhausted the next day with the heat that I was unable to appear at mess. The colonel sent up to find out what was wrong and wanted me to return to the rest camp at once, but I was not sufficiently done up for that, and I only relate this incident to show the thoughtfulness of the commanding officer for those under him.

The next evening after the regiment was relieved the reserves being the last to come out of the trenches, I found a horse waiting for me, on the commanding officer's instructions, so that I would not have the exertion of the march back to camp; that and similar incidents made our affection for our commanding officer a very real thing. But being in reserve had one compensation, in the early morning before the sun rose and just at dawn to lie and watch the wonderful colourings on the Pusht-i-Kuh Hills, colours changing every moment, was always pleasurable, and suddenly a shell would burst near the artillery posi-

Pipe Major Keith.

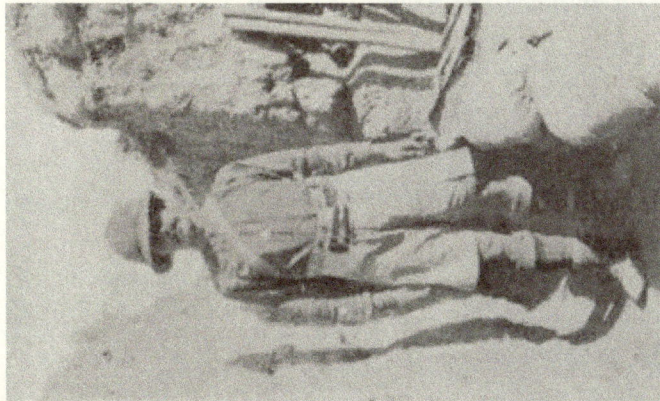

The Regimental Sergeant-major in the Trenches. Sergeant-major A. Smart, M.C.

Quartermaster-sergeant Hobbs.

No. 3 British General Hospital.

tion and one would know the daily Hate and Strafe had started, and shortly after the sun would rise.

We spent some uncomfortable evenings being shelled in these trenches, and watching and waiting for them to burst was not an enjoyable occupation. There were no safe dug-outs to seek safety in, one had to stick it out wherever one was situated and hope for the best. The damage done was seldom great beyond knocking the trenches about a bit and these were soon repaired. Having been put in charge of a digging party one morning in the rearward area whose duty it was to widen and deepen a communication trench, I saw a good opportunity while the work was going on of looking for souvenirs in the shape of Turkish shell caps. So getting out of the trench I commenced a search and continued for some time but without success, when I was driven to seek shelter in the trench by a shell bursting in close proximity, they had evidently spotted someone walking about and opened fire, but it did not last for long.

During our period in the trenches if there was very little doing, as was usually the case during the hot weeks, we were in turn sent down to the Depot three miles behind for two days' rest, and it was an absolute and complete rest. One had nothing whatever to do, get up at any time, go to bed at any time, complete relaxation, those two days were a great boon to us. To have absolutely nothing to do was a great luxury and anything out of the ordinary routine was enjoyable. During my spell of leave at the depot one evening sitting round the mess table which we had outside on account of the great heat, we were discussing the movements of the regiment during the past 20 years and when I remarked that I had watched the regiment embarking at Durban for India 15 years before, the quartermaster said, "I was there and out of the whole battalion that embarked that day, there are only two of us left with the regiment, the sergeant-major and myself".

I little thought as I watched the 2nd Battalion saying farewell to South Africa that 15 years later I would share in some of its trials on the banks of the Tigris. Sitting in the Headquarters Mess in the evening, as I previously stated, one got all the news, about 8 o'clock the quartermaster would appear having come up from the depot in charge of the rations party and to make his report. The mails would be brought up by them too and if the English mail was due and had arrived with letters and papers great was the excitement.

Our letters took about six weeks from England to the firing line, but we were allowed to send weekend cables at a very reduced rate, something like 6d. a word, and could send them off actually from the trenches on their long journey half across the world. The food, taking everything into consideration, was good, although of necessity it had to greatly consist of tinned and dried varieties and we suffered somewhat from lack of fresh vegetables. Later an improvement in this respect was effected.

A flag of truce was always an interesting event. A white flag would be prominently displayed by one side above the trench and kept there till the other side responded and also hoisted a flag, and two or three officers would go out from either side meeting in the middle of "No Man's Land" where the business was discussed. Sometimes it would be simply handing over a letter or letters; other times the business would take longer. A truce of some hours' duration would sometimes be arranged. The longest I remember was for 24 hours when we exchanged sick prisoners; but there was no fraternizing; we might sit on the parapet of our trench and the Turk would do the same; but there was no attempt made to be friendly; the Turk knew and so did we that within a few short months we would be at death grips with each other and that one side or the other would be driven out of the present strong positions we had taken up; but whichever side won, the losses of both would be great and so we sat and looked at each other during those short respites, and both sides adhered strictly to the truce.

When it expired it was not safe to show even a helmet over the parapet. The colonel told me that several times the same Turkish officer brought the flag of truce. He spoke French easily and said he had been fighting more or less continuously the last eight years—in the Iraq against Arabs, in Tripoli against the Italians, in Gallipoli, and now on the Tigris against the British. He had been wounded four times, and was again wounded and taken prisoner by us during the advance, 1917. In 1916 we were fighting a foe, elated by his success at Kut, and it was only after our victories in the spring of 1917, that he showed any signs of war weariness.

One hot and sunny morning I was speaking to one of our sentries who had been watching a Turk appear above their parapet and had already had one shot at him and was waiting to get another and I had scarcely moved a 100 yards down the trench when the unfortunate sentry having looked over too far received a bullet clean through his head. Once or twice during the hot weather bombing parties went over for short raids but without very much success and very little advantage.

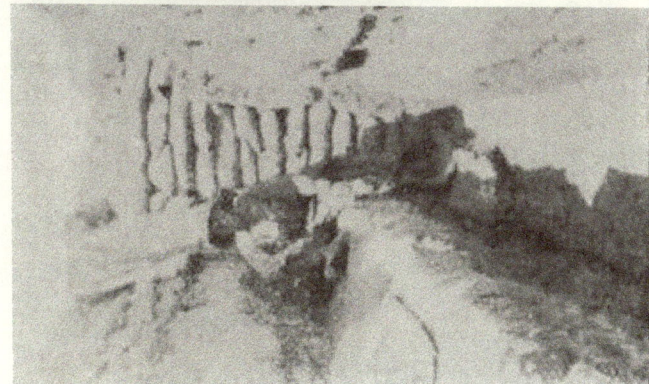

Scenes In The Trenches At San-i-yat.

THE FILTERS.

CAPTAIN MacQUEEN, R.A.M.C., AND HIS AID POST.

Indian Water Carriers At San-i-yat.

I witnessed no instance of gas being used but precautions were taken and gas helmets issued with orders that they must always be carried whilst in the fire zone. Gongs were placed at intervals all along the front line and had to be sounded at the first alarm, but fortunately that alarm never came.

One of my duties was to buy stores for the Officers' Mess and the men's canteen and before Field Force Canteens were opened immediately behind the firing line it meant a trip down to Sheikh Saad about once a month, after the arrival of the canteen boat, of which we were duly notified. Buying was usually brisk but we generally got our fair share of anything going and the regimental canteen retailed to the men at just above cost price, everything was disposed of in a very short space of time as the things for sale were looked upon as luxuries and in great demand.

On the morning of the anniversary of Loos the commanding officer addressed the regiment and proclaimed the day a holiday stating that night a ration of whisky would be issued to commemorate the event. I heard afterwards that it was all the sergeant-major could do to keep the men from cheering, weeks and months had passed since the men had had anything stronger than tea to drink and this ration was much appreciated. Another very welcome event was the arrival of parcels from Lady Carmichael's Gift Fund in Calcutta. A great deal of gratitude is due to Lady Carmichael and her staff and the ladies of India for the way the fund was organised. They sent us shirts and shorts and towels and soap, razors, chocolates, mufflers, cigarettes, tobacco, tinned fruit and *chutney*.

Certainly the best *chutney* I ever tasted came in a gift, I remember it was homemade and came from Assam and the maker's name written on the jar. I told the mess sergeant to write a special letter thanking the maker, thinking that by doing so some more might appear. But I am sorry to have to say, none did. As the summer began to draw to an end preparations had to be made for the winter. The terrific heat of the summer had gone and now the biting cold of winter had to be prepared for. If the coming winter was going to be anything like the previous one, then we were going to suffer; but preparations for it were in full swing.

The Doctor gave an order for a supply of rubber water bottles for his aid post, whereupon a very liberal and kind-hearted officer cabled home for one for each officer. I don't know if anyone else used them for heat purposes. I know I used mine. Fifteen years in tropical cli-

THE REGIMENT IN THE TRENCHES AT SAN-I-YAT.

IN THE SAN-I-YAT TRENCHES

LOOKING TOWARDS THE TURKISH LINES AT SAN-I-YAT.

mates has made the 'cold' one of my worst enemies, but if they were not used as hot water bottles they certainly were as air cushions; this same officer never neglected an opportunity of doing acts of kindness to his brother officers and men immediately under his command, and when he was eventually invalided to India he still remembered his friends and sent them delightful and much appreciated parcels.

QUALAT SALEH.

RAWAL PINDI HOSPITAL, AMARA.

On The Banks of the Tigris.

A Marching Post.

The Bridge at Arab Village.

CHAPTER 6

Attack

Everything was ready. The regiment was in excellent form and fettle, highly trained and efficient, and the powers that be knew that it could be depended on to a man. The first rains had fallen and it was cool without being cold. Mesopotamia takes a long time to cool after the great summer heat and does not usually get very cold till January, and on December 13th the British offensive began on the right bank of the Tigris near Kut, and very severe fighting took place. It was not till February 1917 that the last Turkish position on this bank was captured. In the meantime, on the left bank, the position for the moment remained much the same. Limpits could not cling with greater tenacity to their native rock than the Turks stuck to their position at San-i-yat.

It would seem as if nothing could drive them out from this, the strongest position in Mesopotamia. 'Xmas Day and New Year's Day were spent out of the trenches, but in the forward area. Events were moving rapidly on the other bank, but the marvellous secrecy with which the Commander-in-Chief kept all his plans inspired the greatest confidence in those under him. No one knew his plans; everything was a dead secret; it was even rumoured that his immediate staff were often kept in ignorance up to the last moment, but all ranks had confidence. On January 21st at 4 p.m. we struck camp at Faliyeh, crossed the river and for 10 days occupied a position along the Narrows from Chahela Mounds to near Beit-a-Essa, a distance of about five miles, establishing picquets along the line.

This was a most welcome change. We had been on one side of the river for practically a whole year and new duties and new country broke the monotony. Each Company was divided up. Three companies holding the line along the Tigris bank and the fourth in reserve.

Casualties were very light and Captain Haldane did excellent work sniping and kept the enemy well in hand. The gunners were good enough to remark that a great change was noticeable since the line had been taken over by us; this was probably a little bit of flattery on the part of the artillery men, but it was quite welcome. During these days the commanding officer was an unknown quantity as one never knew where he would next appear on the five-mile line. I think that he must have known every inch of it.

We were relieved by another Highland Regiment and a very pleasant ten days came to an end with a march back across the river to the forward area and back to the now muddy trench at San-i-yat. It was now bitterly cold and uncomfortable at night and the mud in the trench almost as bad as the dust in the summer. Bombardments were of daily occurrence and the Turk must have had a most uncomfortable January. About the middle of February the army commander determined to make a combined attack with one force at the Shumran bend, and with one of our brigades at San-i-yat.

The attack at San-i-yat was delivered by two Indian battalions of our brigade under great disadvantages, and though at first successful, the attackers were eventually compelled to withdraw back to our lines. Every officer and every man regretted that the battalion had not been selected to take part in the attack in the first instance, and were eager to lead the brigade in another assault. This indeed was the wish of the whole brigade, and orders in fact were issued to that effect, but two days later, when every arrangement had been completed, it was decided to make the attack with a fresh brigade and ours was withdrawn and held as a reserve.

Before leaving the trenches, however, the colonel ordered two officer's patrols to go out the last night to examine the enemy's wire and locate, if possible, the position of their machine guns, thinking thus to assist the attack of the coming brigade. Of these patrols one was led by Lieut. Cowie and met with rather exciting adventures. Cowie and two scouts crawled across "No Man's Land" to within 20 yards of the Turkish trench without mishap. Then creeping along the enemy's wire they spotted a machine gun with the team standing beside it. Right into this group the three threw three grenades, wounding several Turks as we afterwards learned. Inevitably the alarm was given, rifle fire broke out in all directions and, before the patrol could make good their escape, Cowie and one of his men were hit.

The Turks saw the two figures lying close to their own wire, jumped

SCENES ON THE
RIVER TIGRIS.

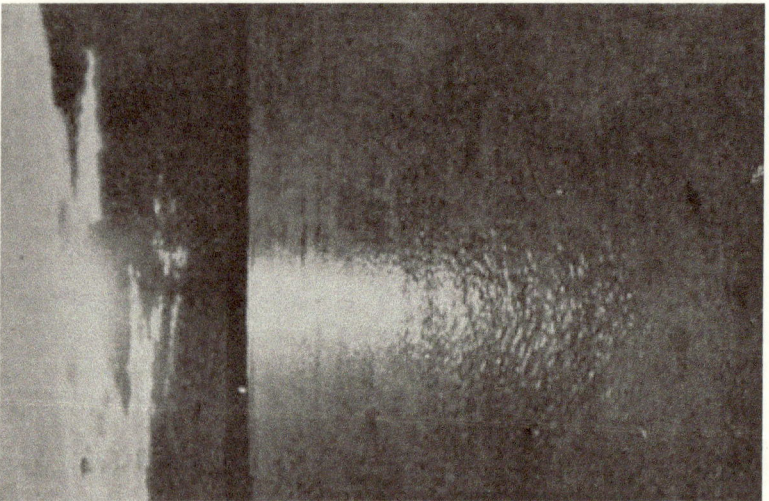

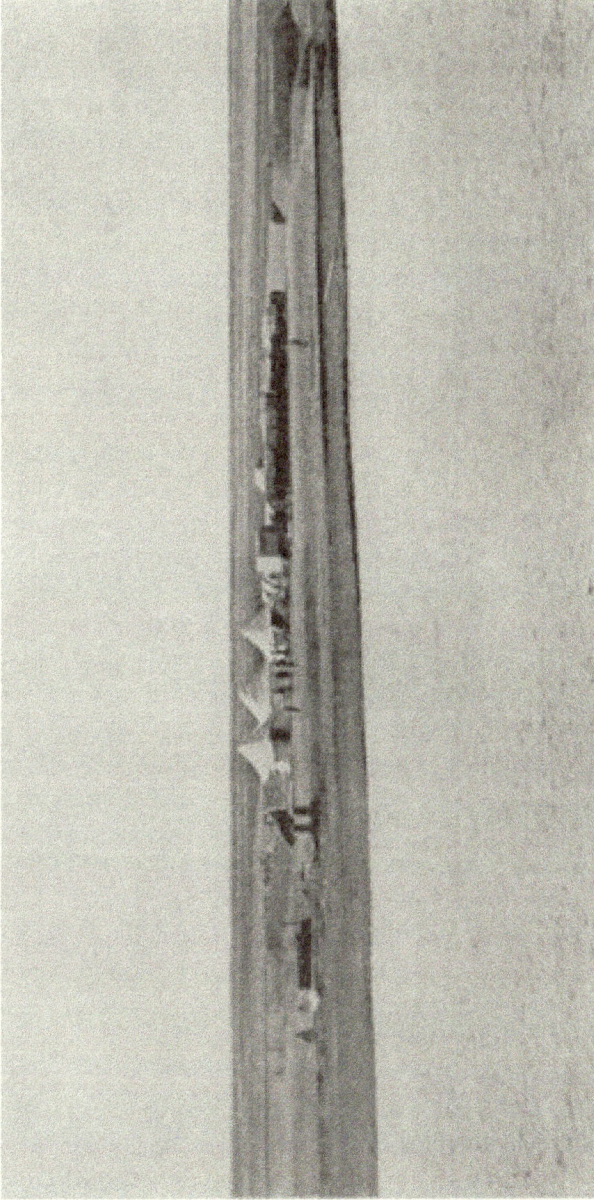

A Post On The Tigris.

the parapet, and made both prisoners, and carried them within their lines. They were well treated, if not well fed, by their captors, and two days later when the retirement began were moved out of the Turkish hospital on to a steamer. This boat was one of two that when trying to escape some days later up the Tigris were captured, after a short but severe engagement, by our gunboats. Cowie, in the confusion of the fight, forced the pilot of his steamer to run her aground and, though most of the Turks effected their escape, Cowie and his orderly instead of continuing their journey to Aleppo, found themselves at General Headquarters attended to by several surgeons and Intelligence Officers, anxious to dress their wounds and hear their story.

On the 22nd the attack was delivered by a battalion of Highlanders and a Punjabi battalion. Under a heavy artillery bombardment they gained the enemy's first line without much loss. Then after severe fighting they captured the enemy's second line and consolidated their position. The Turks made several counter attacks and though nothing could move the Highlanders, the position on the left was not quite secure. Our battalion was therefore ordered back to the trenches, and the colonel obtained leave to send two platoons under Captain Young across to the Turkish position in order to strengthen the left of our new line. Captain Young was wounded, but the two platoons that night and the following day held the line down to the river where a counter attack was most expected.

The colonel asked leave to push forward that day, but it was not till nightfall that two battalions of our brigade were ordered to pass through the other brigade and take the enemy's 4th line. It was necessarily a slow business moving up unknown trenches at night, and the battalion on our left met with considerable resistance. However, if progress was slow it was sure, our patrols pushed steadily forward, the enemy's snipers were forced back and before dawn the whole San-i-yat position was in our hands, and the Turks in full retreat. Thus fell this position which for ten long months had held us up, and had claimed such a big toll of lives from both sides. The sky was clear and without cloud. The same sun shone out on victors as on vanquished, on pursued and pursuers.

One wondered how often, ten months before, the gallant defenders of Kut had looked towards this position longing, hoping, praying for its capture which was only now accomplished. Meanwhile after very hard fighting the Tigris had been bridged at Shumran above Kut and our infantry was pouring across. Patrols of the 2nd Battalion were immediately sent forward towards the Nakhailat position some two miles further east and the two leading companies followed in attack formation. An Indian battalion conformed to our movements on the left, while the leading battalions of the other brigade began to appear on our right rear. None of our men will ever forget the scene that morning, nor the feeling of freedom and elation as our lines passed over trench after trench now deserted by the Turks, and it was these trenches over which we were now so casually advancing that we had been anxiously watching from behind our parapet for nearly a year. It seemed incredible, but we passed by trenches filled with Turkish dead.

We passed several of the heavy *minenwerfers* whose shells had been a source of such trouble and loss the last few months, and before 8 a.m. after some little sniping and the capture of a few prisoners the Nakhailat position was also ours. Here a pause was made by order of the general to give time to another brigade to secure our right flank, and then in conjunction with the Indians on our left the regiment advanced in attack formation with patrols well ahead against the Suwada position, but the crossing of the Shumran Bend the day before had rendered resistance impossible and, after a little firing and the capture of a few more prisoners, the last of the Turkish trenches fell into our hands before noon.

The divisional commander now ordered a halt. An order doubtless necessary, but that was somewhat reluctantly obeyed, the troops being anxious to get in touch with their vanishing foe, and it was not till 4 p.m. that an order came to send two patrols some four miles further north to the Horse Shoe Lake. As it was uncertain what they might encounter the commanding officer sent forward four platoons and they reached the Nwhrwan Ridge without opposition. Our Colonel proposed that the rest of the brigade should push forward after the enemy, but instead of this patrols were brought back about midnight, and it was not till the next day that the line of the Dahra Canal was taken up by the division, the Turks by then being many miles to the north.

On February 24th Kut fell in the hands of the British and the King cabled to the army commander:

> I congratulate you and the troops under your command on the successes recently obtained, and feel confident that all ranks will spare no effort to achieve further success. It is gratifying to me to know that the difficulties of communications which hitherto

hampered your operations have been overcome.

George R.I.

When some five months later I stood on the summit of Kut's famous minaret, from which Briton and Turk had each in their turn observed the enemy closing in on them, and from which one could see the junction of the Hai with the Tigris now very low, the ruins of what was the Liquorice Factory, and miles away Es Sinn and San-i-yat, it was impossible not to be impressed and to feel a certain sadness and yet a great admiration for all those lives which had been so freely given to uphold the honour of the flag and the dignity of the Empire, and how when failure after failure had dogged our steps, grit and perseverance had at last won the day, and success crowned our efforts. Kut was ours; it must have cheered those lonely prisoners in captivity in the fastnesses of Asia Minor when the news eventually leaked through that their defeat was avenged and that the flag which Townshend had been compelled to haul down once again flew over the small but famous village to the Banks of the Tigris.

Pursuing is only slightly less arduous than being pursued, and in his despatches well might the army commander have quoted those famous words used centuries before by another great leader when an equally strenuous pursuit was in progress. 'Faint yet pursuing'. One has to remember that these same troops had been cooped up in trenches for nearly a year, and to suddenly be called upon to take a prominent part in such a pursuit as was now in progress was no ordinary strain. Not a man in No. 1. Platoon fell out on the march from San-i-yat to Baghdad, a record of which the platoon and its officer might well be proud. The going was bad, there was no road as one understands a road in England, it was plain flat open country. A stay was made at Dahra and then a night march carried us to Shumran, where there were signs of a cavalry fight and prisoners were being brought in.

The brigade had orders to clear the battlefield and booty of all kinds, guns and ammunition were collected, rifles which had been thrown away, as it is easier to run without one than with, and what little surplus kit the Turk possessed had been discarded, so that his flight might not be impeded; they were all out for Baghdad and we were all out after them, but we were out-running our Transport and Supplies, and the meals during the great pursuit were both scanty and irregular, but who cared, so long as we had enough to carry us on.

All England was looking on, and day by day following our progress

B. H. Lunn and C. V. Hendry.

Lunn has a quiet rest and Smoke.

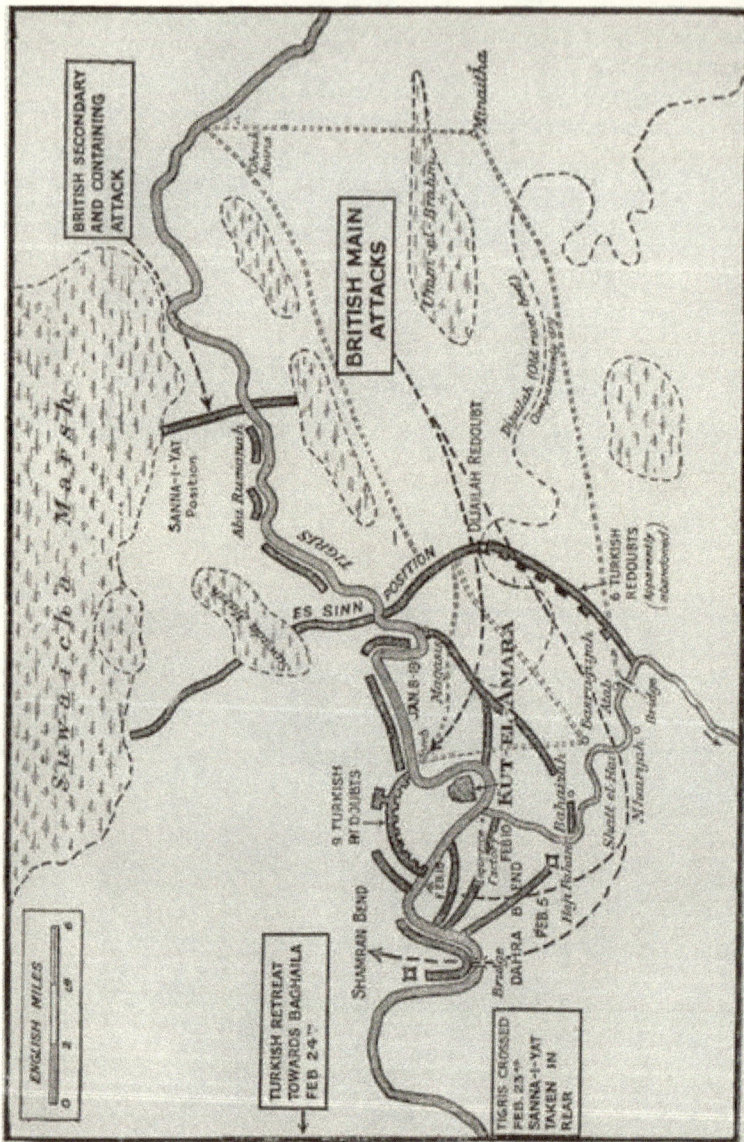

MAP: THE OPERATIONS AT KUT-EL-AMARA, SHOWING THE WIDE TURNING MOVEMENTS SOUTH OF THE RIVER.

with feverish interest. "Is Baghdad going to be taken" was on everyone's lips. Beards were making their appearance even on the youngest soldiers' chins, numbers of men were being knocked up by the continuous strain and a four days' halt was called at Sheik Jaad, No. 1 Company being sent forward to Beghailah. Still pressing forward we reached Azizie, 46 miles from Baghdad, and the total number of prisoners since the advance now mounted to well over 5,000. Turkish depots and stores at many points were in flames, 38 guns, many machine guns, trench mortars, ships, tugs and barges, miscellaneous river craft and bridging material fell into our hands.

Booty was strewn over 80 miles of country and the Arabs living in the neighbourhood must have secured sufficient goods of various description to last them the rest of their lives.

Zeur, Bustan, then Ctesiphon were all passed, there being no time or opportunity to stay and examine the famous arch. But as we halted for the night beside the magnificent ruin, one could but reflect on the ironies of a soldier's fortune. Here it was, long before the arch was built, that the Emperor Julian, marching from Constantinople, had been forced to halt his army, and met with disaster and death; and under the ruins of this great arch Townshend, advancing from Basra, had engaged in the battle that eventually brought his division to disaster and captivity. And now Maude, encamped for the night beside the ancient city walls, was pressing forward with his whole force to the capture of Baghdad and Samarra.

The next morning, the 9th of March, we were glad of a short march to Bawi. The division crossed the Tigris by a pontoon bridge that night; our brigade being in reserve. After a hard march we reached Shawa Khan, the enemy retiring before us and our brigade came under shell fire only. The following day was a very trying one. A gale was blowing right in our faces, and the dust was so thick that our movements on that day resembled some horrible night march. We manoeuvred the whole day, and twice the orders for attack were cancelled owing to the difficulty of gaining contact with the enemy. Towards evening we struck the Euphrates-Baghdad Railway and were preparing to attack when orders came postponing further movements till midnight.

Never had any of us experienced such a dust storm. With great difficulty we brought up the 2nd Line Transport, filled the men's water bottles, and formed a brigade bivouac. Movement was again postponed till 3 a.m. on account of the storm, though some of us thought

DIFFERENT TYPES OF BOATS ON THE TIGRIS.

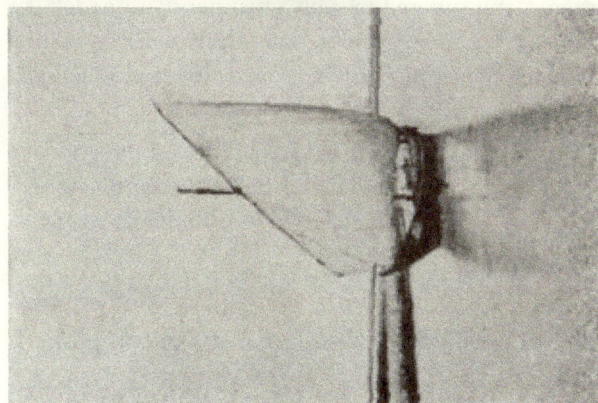

SAILING BOATS ON THE TIGRIS.

it had been better to take advantage of the darkness and make the attack at once. At 3 a.m. our patrols were sent forward, the battalion following in artillery formation. Right well led, the patrols pushed on meeting with no real resistance.

When about a mile short of the Iron Bridge that crosses the Kharr Canal, the colonel received a message that our leading patrol had gained the railway station in Baghdad before 6 a.m., that no Turks remained, and that we were driving out the Arabs with little difficulty. This information was immediately sent back to the army commander, and the Red Haeckle was the first British emblem seen in Baghdad. The medical officer of the battalion observing a Turkish flag flying over a building, quickly climbed up and hauled it down. That flag is now a trophy of the regiment.

The Turks had fled, but all that morning firing continued both in the town and neighbouring palm groves, caused chiefly by Arabs and Kurds shooting and looting in all directions. The brigade, under General Thompson, had the well deserved honour of marching through the city, and order and confidence was soon established. The regiment took an outpost position on the north of the City towards Kadhimain, and very pleasant was the rest under the shade of the palm groves.

The fall of Baghdad was a severe blow not only to the Turks but to the whole Quadruple Alliance, but how many who read that cheering and inspiring news on the morning of March 12th thought of the trials endured and overcome, thought of the sacrifices and losses that had been endured to make that news possible. How many knew of the advance in the blinding dust storm, when men gasped for air and water. How many knew of the fight on the Dialah when the Lancashires covered themselves with glory; these things are not always published but they were suffered, and suffered in such a manner that one felt it a privilege to belong to the same regiment, division or army, and when the congratulatory message from the King, our colonel in chief, was read to the different regiments:

It is with the greatest satisfaction that I have received the good news that you have occupied Baghdad. I heartily congratulate you and your troops on their success achieved under so many difficulties,

One knew that the Head of all our race understood and appreciated all that had been endured suffered, and accomplished.

On board a Paddle Boat going up the Tigris.

Kurnah, supposed site of the Garden Of Eden.
124° in shade when this was taken.

Waiting for another boat to pass.

BAGHDAD AS IT EXISTS TODAY.

DRAWN FROM PHOTOGRAPHS AND A PLAN PROVIDED BY THE NATIONAL ELECTRIC CONSTRUCTION COMPANY, LIMITED.

CHAPTER 7

The Battle Beyond Baghdad

By Brigadier-general A. G. Wauchope, C.M.G., D.S.O.

The following chapter appeared in *Blackwoods Magazine* for August 1917:—

On the banks of the Tigris I am lying in the shadow of a palm, looking down the river on the brick walls and mud roofs, on the mosques and minarets of the city of Baghdad, and as I look I am lost in wonder. For although I am now lying in a grove of date-palms, it is fifteen months since I have seen a tree of any kind; it is fifteen months since I have seen a house or lain under a roof; and this girl coming towards me with hesitating steps, clothed in rags and patches, this little date-seller with her pale face and dark eyes, her empty basket resting on her small, well-shaped head—this is the first woman I have seen or spoken to for more than a year.

Perhaps it is the twilight which gives a feeling of mystery and beauty unknown in the glare and noise of midday, and I hardly know, as the Tigris seems to lose itself in the evening mists, above which the golden minarets of Kazimain still shine and glitter in the setting sun, whether I am truly in the land of reality or if I still linger but half awake in the realm of dreams and fancies, where stand the gates of horn and ivory.

For to how many during the past two years has not flashed the dream of the capture of this city, Dar-al-Salam, the City of Security? And of those who have seen the vision, how many have wondered from which gate the dream has issued, and how many have been filled with confidence? For that vision has drawn many thousands from Basrah and Amarah—many who are now here in the hour of victory,

119

THE TRANSPORT OFFICER.

CAPTAIN R. MacFARLANE, M.C.
KILLED IN ACTION.

Arabs bargaining on the Tigris Banks with troops going up river. A brisk trade is done in eggs and fowls.

many who now lie where they fell on the field of battle, and many who are still prisoners and captives.

A few days ago, as the columns of the Army of Mesopotamia were hurrying past the great Arch of Ctesiphon, it was impossible not to think of the *7th (Meerut)* Division arriving there some eighteen months earlier—that gallant *7th (Meerut)* Division, war-worn and depleted in numbers but ever victorious, who found at Ctesiphon, in the hour of their last and most glorious victory, the beginning of their undoing and tragic end.

What dream was it of a captured city, of a City of Security, that lured them to their doom, and who was the first dreamer? And who next saw the second dream of fresh battalions and a new organisation that would lead without fail to Baghdad, and had the gift to know that this dream, unlike the other, had passed through the gate of horn?

So I mused but a week ago in the palm groves that had been ringing that very morning with rifle-shots, but seemed so quiet and peaceful in the evening light that I felt all the rush of the past pursuit was over, that our efforts had not only been crowned with success, but that a period of rest would now be given to man and beast. For the pursuit had been much more than merely a hot and dusty march of 120 miles from San-i-yat to Baghdad.

All through January and February the army commander had been preparing the way by a series of small victories which gradually drove the Turks, holding the right bank of the Tigris, across the Shatt-al-Hai, and a dozen miles above Kut. Then came the combined master-stroke on February 22 and 23. First, on the 22nd, came the successful attack on the San-i-yat trenches—the position that had held us at bay for a twelve month—the position that had finally checked our troops, struggling most bravely, but struggling in vain, for the relief of their comrades in Kut. This success drew several Turkish battalions to the help of the San-i-yat garrison, and so weakened the Turkish line elsewhere. And then at dawn, on the 23rd, came the crossing of the Tigris five miles above the Shatt-al-Hai—a crossing that will remain famous in history—when the bravery of the troops will not make one forget the careful preparation of the commander and his skill in making success possible, by causing the Turk to mass his troops both above and below the actual point selected for crossing.

This well-timed and brilliantly executed stroke had sent the Turk flying; but though in the two months' fighting he had lost over 8,000 in prisoners and more than that number in killed and wounded, he was still able to fight a series of stubborn rearguard actions before the road was free to Baghdad. It was dawn on the 11th of March before the Highlanders, who were leading, reached the city, and an order to rest and be thankful had been welcome to troops more used to trench warfare than constant rapid marching in the open.

But when airmen brought intelligence that the enemy was holding an entrenched position some twenty miles north of the city, it was obvious that some of us must move upriver and drive him back.

It was once remarked by an American officer, who had served throughout the Civil War, that he knew that every soldier in the army was always longing to be in the next battle. He knew this because it was so said by every general and so written by every newspaper editor. And yet, although he had served in several regiments during the war, he had always found that that particular itch was more lively in neighbouring units than in his own.

So when orders arrived on the 13th of March for our division to advance that night, our friends from other divisions congratulated us with what seemed almost undue heartiness on our good fortune in being selected, and the estimate of the numbers of the opposing Turks rose rapidly from five thousand to fifteen thousand. However, the estimated number finally settled down to about half that, with thirty guns, and these figures were subsequently substantiated by captured prisoners.

These orders put an end to the peaceful enjoyment of the palm grove, and preparations were hurried forward. Blankets and waterproof sheets were all stacked, men and officers all carried their own great coats and rations for the next day, water-bottles were filled that afternoon, and enough water was carried on mules to refill them once the next day, and no more given to man or animal till the morning of the 15th. This should be borne in mind when judging of the difficulties overcome by the troops in this action, for the shade temperature on the 14th was about 80°, and there was no shade.

The Turk certainly had judged it impossible for us to advance so far from the river, for we learned later that he had laid out the trace of most of his trenches between the river and the railway; but our main attack was delivered west of the railway, a success there forcing the withdrawal of the whole of his line.

Save for several severe dust-storms the whole pursuit had been blessed with fine weather, and it was on a beautiful starlit night that our division formed up along the railway for the march towards

EZRA'S TOMB.

AN ARAB VILLAGE.

Fishing by net on the Tigris.

Arabs selling produce on the banks of the river.

On the banks of the Tigris.

Mushaidie, a station some twenty miles north of Baghdad on the direct road to Berlin.

Night marches, the text-book says, may be made for several reasons, but it does not suggest that one of these ever could be for pleasure. Constant and unexpected checks break the swing that counts so much for comfort on a long march; hurrying on to make up for lost ground, stumbling in rough places, belated units pushing past to the front, whispered but heated arguments with staff officers, all threaten the calm of a peaceful evening and also that of a well-balanced mind.

Many a soldier sadly misses his pipe, which, of course, may not be lit on a night march; but to me a greater loss is the silence of those other pipes, for the sound of the bagpipes will stir up a thousand memories in a Highland regiment, and nothing helps a column of weary foot-soldiers so well as pipe-music, backed by the beat of drum. This march was neither better nor worse than its fellows, and we had covered some fourteen miles before we halted at dawn. Then we lay down, gnawed a biscuit, tasted the precious water in our bottles, and waited for what news airmen would bring of the enemy.

The day is not wasted on which one has seen the sun rise—perhaps some of us changed the old saying, and felt the day would be well spent for him who saw the sun set,—for in war, however sure the victory, so also is the toll of killed and wounded, and the attack of an enemy entrenched in this country, as bare and open as the African *veld*, is done readily, gladly, but not without losses; and the time one thinks of these is not in the charge, not in the advance, but in the empty period of waiting beforehand. The needle pricks before, not during, the race. "Remember only the happy hours," and if the most glorious hour in life is the hour of victory in battle, so are the hours preceding battle among the most depressing. I confess, as we sat there idle in the chill dawn, my mind was filled not only with the hope of victory and captured trenches, but with memories of past scenes in France and Mesopotamia, and of a strip of ground the evening after Magersfontein, each battlefield dotted with little groups of men lying rigid, each marked with lines of motionless forms.

Action quickly dispels such thoughts, and we all welcomed the definite news that was at last brought of the enemy, and our orders for a farther advance. One brigade was immediately sent forward on the east side of the railway in order to press back the advanced parties of the enemy on their main position, some six miles north of our present halting place. A brave sight it is to see a brigade deploying for action.

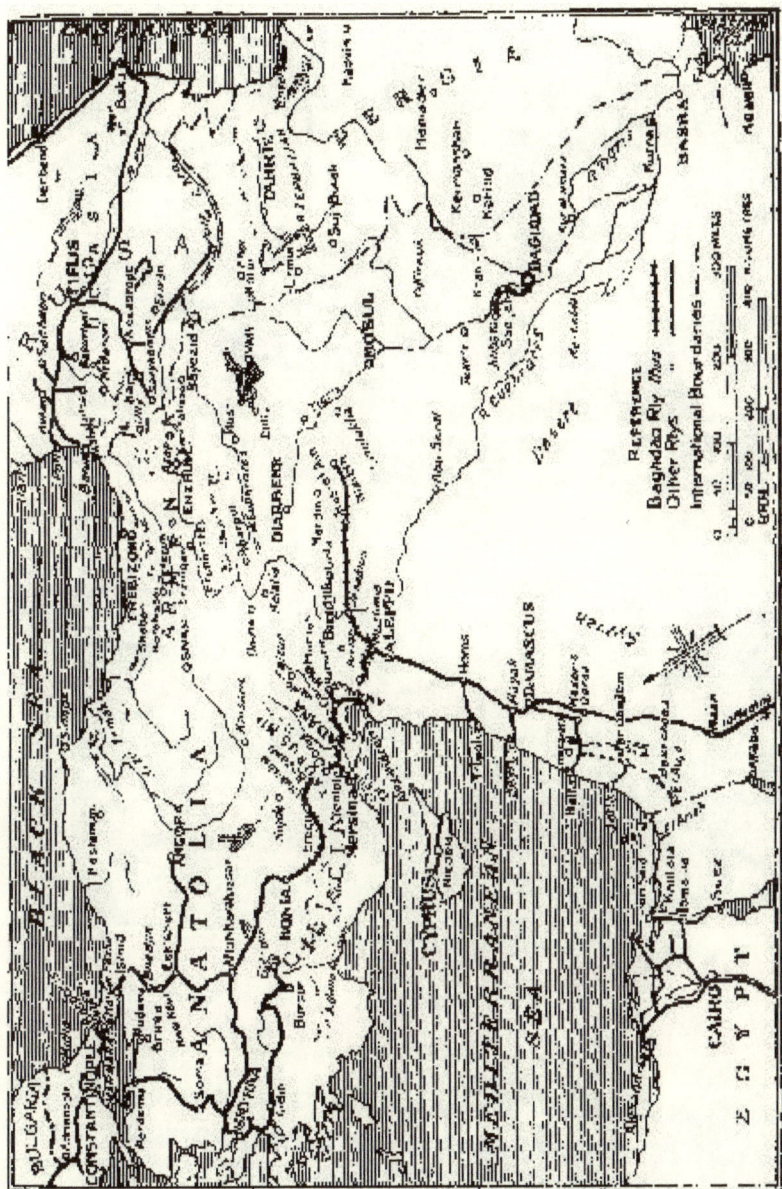

THE COURSE OF THE BAGHDAD RAILWAY.

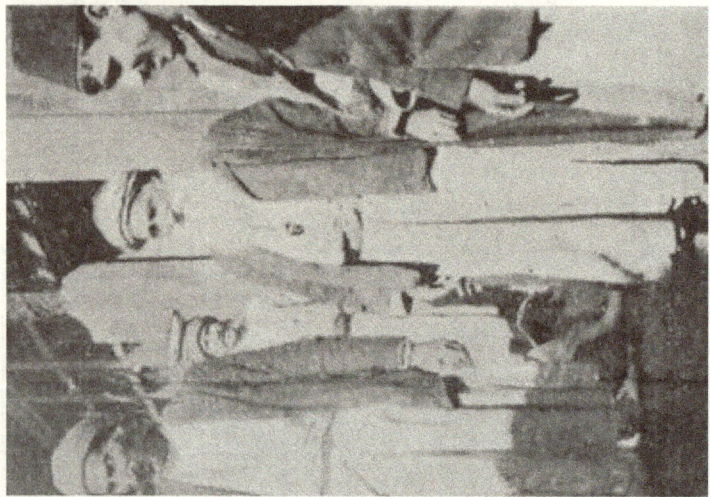

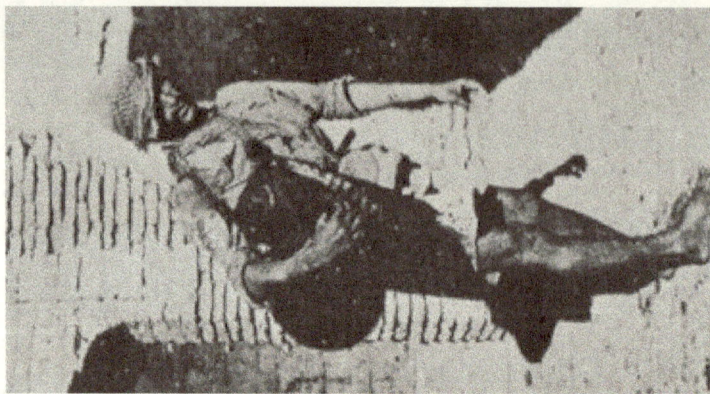

Different Types in Mesopotamia.

Even though the scarlet doublet has given place to the khaki jacket, though no pipes sound and no colours are unfurled, the spirit still remains; the spirit that in old days led the British line to victory still fills these little columns scattered at wide intervals over the plain, these little columns of Englishmen, Highlanders, Indians, and Gurkhas.

The brigade pushed forward for a mile or two without opposition, then little puffs of white smoke bursting in the air showed that the Turk had opened the battle with salvoes of shrapnel; the little columns quickly spread out into thin lines, and our batteries trotted forward and were soon themselves engaged in action. So far the scene had been clear in every detail, but now as the day advanced, the dust from advancing batteries, the smoke and mirage, formed a fog of war that telephones and signallers could only in part dispel.

The mirage in Mesopotamia does not so much hide as distort the truth. The enemy are seldom altogether hidden from view, the trouble is rather to tell whether one is observing a cavalry patrol or an infantry regiment, or if the object moving forward is not in reality a sandhill or a bunch of reeds. The mirage here has certainly a strange power of apparently raising objects above the ground-level. I remember well from a camp near Falahiyah the Sinn Banks, which are perhaps thirty feet above the plain, were quite invisible in the clear morning air, but about noon they were easy to distinguish as a cloudy wall swaying to and fro in the distant haze. Nor shall I forget the instance of an officer who once assured me he had observed five Arab horsemen within a mile of our column: we rode forward, and soon the five shadowy horsemen gave place to five black crows hopping about by the edge of the Suwaicha marsh.

But the most curious illusion I have seen in this way was looking towards the Pusht-i-Kuh hills across the marsh from San-i-yat. The foothills, some thirty miles distant, had sometimes the appearance of ending in abrupt white cliffs such as one sees at Dover. The cause of this was a great number of dead fish which had been stranded as the marsh receded, and their white bellies, a mile away, gave the appearance of white cliffs to the base of the Persian hills, which in reality slope very gradually down to the level of the Tigris valley.

So in Mesopotamian battles, little can be trusted that is seen, and to gain information of the enemy commanders are bound to rely on reports by aeroplane, messengers, and telephones.

The battle now before us was to be fought over ground typical of the Tigris valley and the desert into which it merges. There are

ARAB GIRL LABOURERS.

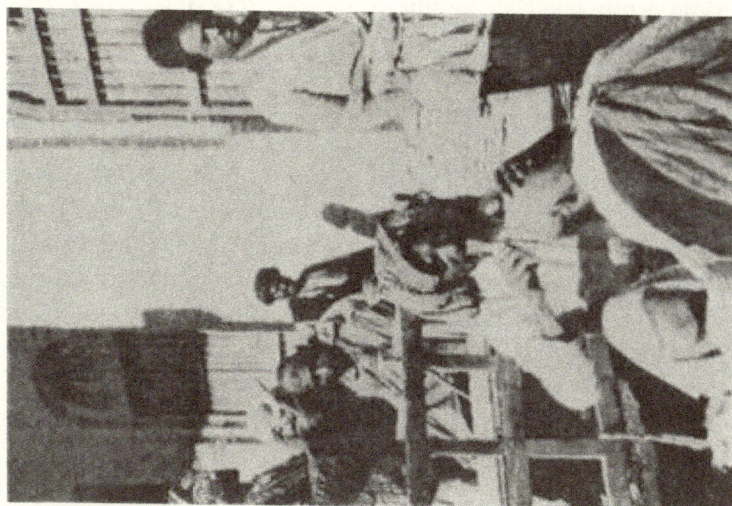

The Barber.

Washing Clothes.

no hills, trees, or any distinguishing features, but the strip nearest the river, varying from one to several miles in breadth, is cultivated and intersected with irrigation channels, some six feet, some six inches, in width and depth. These are invaluable as cover to troops on the defensive, and almost impassable to transport carts.

It was here the enemy had expected us, and was holding numerous trenches between the river and the railway; but our commanders wisely waited till their information was complete, and then decided to make our main attack on the enemy's extreme right, some six miles from the river. The ground in this part is a wide open desert, bare and level except for a few low sandhills; but in the dips and hollows below the sandhills the khaki-coloured desert changes into a thick growth of fresh green grass, dotted with countless daisies and dandelions, and a little white flower resembling alyssum giving a sweet smell to all the countryside. Some five miles beyond our halting-place a definite ridge runs east and west across the railway, and ends in a low sugar-loaf hill about forty feet high. This ridge was reported to be entrenched and held by the Turk, and this ridge we were ordered to attack and capture.

Our first brigade had moved forward on the east side of the railway, but had been eventually held up mainly by enfilade artillery fire coming from positions stretching nearer to the river than to the railway. The whole brigade was now lying stretched out in extended order some three thousand yards ahead of us, with the left regiment touching the railway embankment. Our brigade had followed for some miles in their tracks, but was now ordered to cross to the western side of the railway by a small culvert and form up for the main attack some three or four miles south of the enemy's position. This was done without difficulty, the third brigade of our Division being held in support on our left rear.

After the orders and dispositions had been explained to every man, magazines were charged, and the Highland regiment deployed into attack formation in four lines of half-platoons in file. A battalion of Gurkhas was deployed on our left, and the third battalion of the brigade was formed up in rear of the Gurkhas. The main attack was thus to be delivered on a narrow front of five hundred yards, the machine-gun company being held in readiness to support the assaulting battalions as occasion offered. The first-line transport with the reserve ammunition halted near the culvert through which we had crossed the railway, but both our reserve ammunition and our Aide Post were brought forward as the attack developed.

At 3.30 p.m. we advanced, and soon had passed the two field batteries covering our front, and reached, without opposition, the lines of the first brigade extended on the east side of the railway. About four o'clock our patrols reported that the enemy was holding not only the main ridge that joins Sugar Loaf Hill with the railway embankment, but also a broken line of low sandhills a few hundred yards in front of the main position. At the same time some shrapnel burst over our leading platoons, and a party of Turks, directly on our left, opened long-range rifle fire. The battalion halted under cover of some sandhills, the final orders were issued, and half a company and two machine-guns were sent to clear the enemy firing from our left flank.

Happily the latter retired at once when fired on, and the battalion advanced in perfect order, the small columns extending into line as the enemy's rifle fire grew more and more severe. The Turkish batteries now kept up a regular fire of both shrapnel and high-explosive shell, but these detonated badly, and our losses on this account were small. A *rafale* of shrapnel will of course destroy any infantry moving in the open, but intermittent shelling, although it appears to be terribly destructive, will not stop resolute troops determined to press forward. But the farther we advanced the more evident it became that Sugar Loaf Hill was the key of the position. It stood seven or eight hundred yards west of the railway, and the enemy's riflemen from the entrenchments on top brought a deadly enfilade fire to bear on our advancing lines.

The Gurkhas moving in *echelon* on our left escaped this, but to meet it and to dominate the enemy's fire, the Highlanders were compelled to extend to the left, their supporting platoons being used to fill up the gap. Two machine-gun sections also pressed gallantly forward, and in spite of continual and heavy losses from now onwards, did much to help us to gain superiority of fire over the enemy.

The battle was now divided into two parts. On our left the Turks had been forced to retire from their advanced positions, but on the right they still held some trenches among the broken ground near the railway, two hundred yards in advance of the main position on the ridge; but on the right our losses had not been so severe, nor was our line so extended.

On the left the Turk occupied no advanced positions, but he outflanked our line, and the enfilade fire from his commanding positions was causing such losses that it seemed impossible for our men to con-

Indian Cavalry watering at Arab village.

Landing stores at Arab village.

The Great Bund built to keep back the marsh at Falahiyah.

THE LIQUORICE FACTORY, KUT.

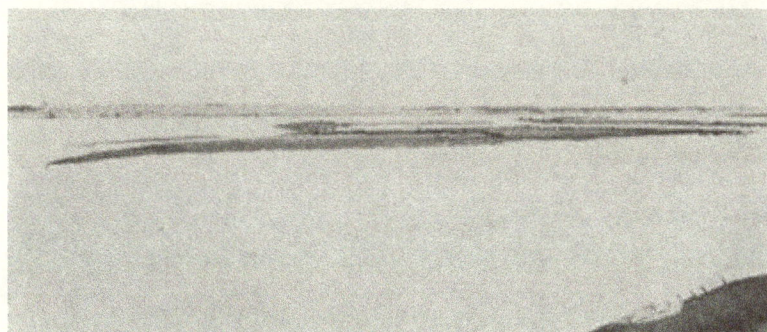

THE RIVER AT KUT.

DRAWING WATER AT KUT.

VIEW FROM THE KUT MINARET TOWARDS THE HAI.

KUT.

PROGRESS IS BEING MADE AT KUT, IT NOW HAS ITS MUNICIPALITY.

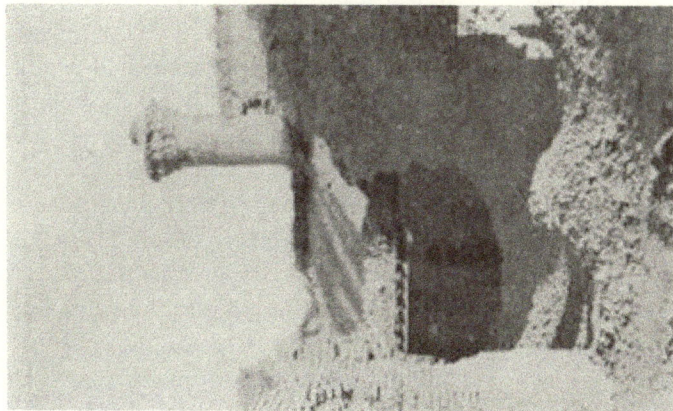

THE KUT MINARET.

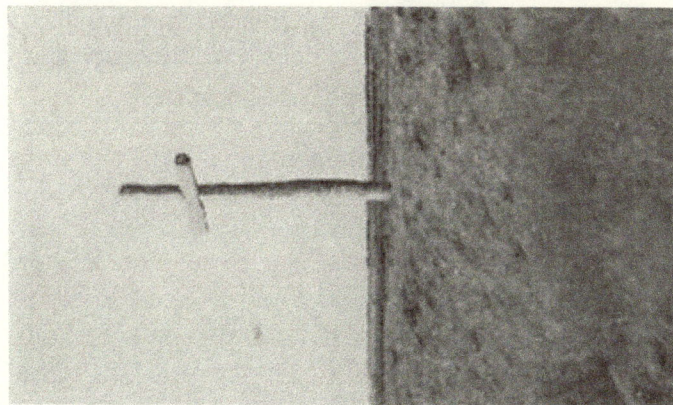

LOOKING TOWARDS KUT.

TOWNSHEND'S TRENCHES, KUT.

tinue the advance without strong artillery support. Unfortunately this was not forthcoming at the time, because our covering batteries had found they were at extreme range, and were now in the act of moving to a more forward position. If an attacking line wavers and halts within close range of an enemy entrenched, that attack is *done* until supports come up and give it again an impetus forward. But there were now few supports available, and the moment most critical.

Yet all along our front small sections of Highlanders still continued to rise up, make a rush forward, and fling themselves down, weaker perhaps by two or three of their number, but another thirty yards nearer the enemy. Now the last supports pressed into the firing line, and as one leader fell, another took his place. One platoon changed commanders six times in as many minutes, but a lance-corporal led the remaining men with the same dash and judgment as his seniors.

It was at this time our Lewis gun teams lost so heavily. The weight of the gun and the extra ammunition carried renders their movements slower than that of their comrades, and consequently the teams offer a better target as well as one specially sought for by the enemy. The officer in charge, Lieutenant Gillespie, had brought up two of our guns in the endeavour to subdue the fire from Sugar Loaf Hill, but at the very moment of giving the range his left arm was shattered. He had been light-weight champion of India, and as he now continued fighting, I could not but compare him to his famous predecessor in the Ring, who carried on the fight with one arm broken. I know those brave, brown eyes of his never flinched in pain, nor wavered in doubt, as he made his way back, not to the Aide Post, but in order to bring forward two more guns for the same purpose. But, alas! while directing their fire he was seen by some Turkish riflemen and fell, never again to rise, his breast pierced by two bullets.

A number of staff and artillery officers witnessed this attack by a Highland regiment. Some were chiefly impressed by so much individual gallantry, others at the example of what can be achieved by collective determination. Was it the result of hard and constant training, perfect discipline, or *esprit de corps* that at this moment of trial made these thin extended lines work as if by clockwork to their own saving and the victory of our arms?

It was during this advance of five hundred yards that the regiment met with its heaviest losses. With four officers and half his men killed or wounded, and an enemy machine-gun pouring a continuous stream of bullets on to the remainder, the situation is not a happy one for a

THE ASSISTANT ADJUTANT.

CAPTAIN W. A. YOUNG,
COMMANDING No. 2 COMPANY

The Money Changer

company sergeant-major, and this was the situation which the young Sergeant-Major Ben Houston of our left company had now to face. He turned round, as so often in battle one does turn round, hoping to see supports pushing forward, and a bullet seared an ugly line across both shoulders. Without waiting, he led his men on, and another bullet struck his bayonet; fragments cut his face and made his eye swell, so that he could not see out of it. Yet when I met him at midnight after the last charge, he told me much of the battle and nothing of his wounds. High praise is due to those who, although weakened by wounds, continue fighting and undertaking fresh responsibilities.

The company next on the left fared little better, but these two companies forced the enemy back, and occupied the low sandhills some two hundred yards in advance of his main position, and there waited, by order, before making the final assault. The left company lost two signallers killed, and the next company had four signallers all wounded in the act of calling for more ammunition. Ammunition was brought up, but, though many brave men fell and many brave deeds were done, nothing was carried out with greater bravery, nothing contributed more to our success, than the maintenance of communication throughout the battle.

The left half battalion, reduced to less than half of its original numbers, was in need of help. This help it now gained from the action of the companies on the right. Undismayed by the enemy shell and rifle fire, these two companies, gallantly assisted by the Indian battalion on the east side of the railway, pressed forward, and at five o'clock charged the enemy, and drove him out of his advanced trenches at the point of the bayonet. The very quickness of the manoeuvre had ensured its success, though it was only achieved with considerable loss to ourselves as well as to the Turk. But the gain was great.

Small parties of Highlanders now crept forward among the sanddunes, two Lewis guns were taken to the east side of the railway embankment, and a hot enfilade fire was brought to bear on the enemy main position. So effective was this that the Turks were forced to evacuate the ridge for some 400 yards nearest the railway, and even from Sugar Loaf Hill his fire weakened, and the relief to our left half battalion and to the Gurkhas was correspondingly great. Streams of wounded Turks were also seen passing from the ridge to the rear: it was not only the British who suffered losses on the 14th of March.

The situation was now greatly in our favour, and it only wanted a final charge to complete the success. But this assault could not be

No. 1 Company prepares for Inter-company
Cross-country Run.

Highland Games on the Tigris Front.

The last meal in camp.

THE MEN'S FIELD KITCHEN.

STAFF OF OFFICERS' MESS AT SAN-I-YAT.

LOADING UP THE KITS.

made without either artillery support or the arrival of fresh troops to fill up our depleted and extended ranks. Our colonel, therefore, ordered all companies to wait in the positions they had gained, but to be ready to charge immediately after the batteries had bombarded the enemy trenches. Consequently, during the next hour both sides remained on the defensive.

Little ironies pursue us through life; in battle Death sometimes comes with a touch so swift and so ironical that we are made to fear God truly.

Englishmen have learned now the meaning of the saying, dear to the French soldier, "*de ne pas s'en faire,*" and in the lull of battle before the bombardment, Sergeant Strachan and Cleek Smith talked of old times. There had been nine Strachans in the regiment when we landed in France two and a half years ago, one of whom was then my orderly. "Any news this morning?" I would sometimes ask.—

"Nothing much, sir, only another of the Strachans was killed last night."

My orderly had become a sergeant, but the other eight were no longer with the battalion. They had all left, "on command."

"Yes," said Cleek Smith, "I wonder why it is so many poor chaps get it the minute they join the regiment, while fellows like you and me go through one show after another and never get a scratch."

Scarce a bullet was fired during that half-hour, yet as a full stop to his question came one that found a way to that gallant heart, which had never failed him in the most critical fight, nor on the most dangerous duty when out scouting. Cleek Smith, you know the answer now to an even greater Riddle than the one you put to the last of the Strachans. No man liveth unto himself, and whoever dies in battle, dies for his regiment, his country, and the cause.

The telephone plays an important part in open warfare, as it does in the trenches, and though the brigade signalling officer and many of his men were killed, intermittent communication was kept up throughout the battle between the battalion, the covering batteries, and the brigade commander. The value of this was now extreme. By telephone our colonel communicated his intentions to the firing line, and thus prevented those sporadic attacks by independent platoons, at once so gallant, so ineffective, and so deadly in losses. By telephone he explained the situation to the brigadier, who ordered up half a battalion of another Highland regiment, old friends of ours, but never more wanted than now, and by telephone he arranged that the batteries should bombard as heavily as possible the trenches on the right of Sugar Loaf Hill, the bombardment to begin at 6.25 and to last for six minutes.

During this hour rifle fire grew less and less, artillery firing ceased. High above the battlefield some crested larks were singing, even as they sing on a quiet evening over the trenches in France, as they sing over the fields at home. A few green and bronze bee-eaters hovered almost like hawks over the sand-dunes, and a cloud of sandgrouse were swinging and swerving across the open ground that divided Highlander from Turk. The wind had died quite away, and a scent of alyssum filled the air. There was no movement among the troops, there was none even among the slender wild grasses of the plain. The sun, that had been blazing all through the day, now hung low in the western sky.

The sound of battle was dying, even as the day was dying. "The world was like a nun, breathless in adoration." And we soldiers, absorbed in this remote corner of the world war, intent on the hour immediately before us, lay there breathless in expectancy. Suddenly our 18-pounders opened gun fire. With rare precision shrapnel burst all along the enemy trenches, and at 6-30, as the shelling slackened in intensity, the Highlanders rose as one man, their bayonets gleaming in the setting sun, and, with the Gurkhas on their left, rushed across the open. There was little work for the bayonet. The Turk fled as our men closed, and the position so long and hardly fought for was won.

The Highlanders had gained their objective, but had lost heavily in officers and men. The remainder were exhausted by the labours of the past twenty-four hours and by lack of water; but when orders came to push forward and capture Mushaidie railway station there was no feeling of doubt or hesitation. Some time was spent in re-organisation, in bringing up and distributing reserve ammunition; the two left companies were amalgamated, and an officer detailed to act with the right wing of the Gurkhas, since that battalion, though it had not suffered such heavy losses in men, had only two officers left unwounded. The two companies of the supporting Highland battalion now arrived and were detailed as a reserve to our attacking line.

The Third Regiment of our brigade had been operating far out on the left flank, and were now occupying Sugar Loaf Hill, from which they had driven the last remaining Turks, and the Indian regiment on the right of the railway, which had fought so well with us throughout the battle, received orders to halt for the night.

SERGEANT-MAJOR I. E. NIVEN.

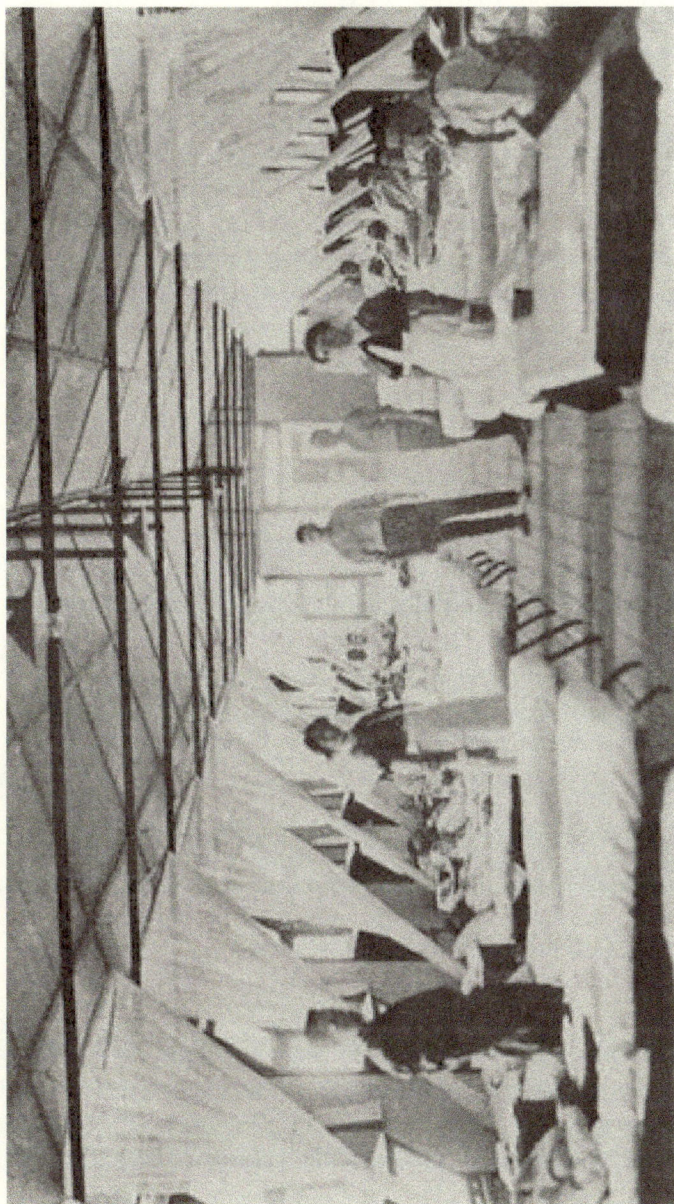

INTERIOR OF A HOSPITAL WARD IN MESOPOTAMIA.

And thus we advanced alone; but though hungry, thirsty, weary, worn, there was full confidence among all ranks, and one resolve united all—the determination to press forward and complete the rout of the enemy.

A mile ahead we passed a position, strongly entrenched but luckily deserted by the Turks, and it was not for another two miles, when our patrols came close to the station, that the enemy was reported in any numbers. There the patrols described a scene of considerable confusion. A train was shunting, and many Turks rushing about and shouting orders. Our patrols were working half a mile ahead of the regiment, so in spite of every effort it was half an hour later before we filed silently past the station, formed up once again for the attack, and charged with the bayonet. The enemy fired a few shots, one of our men and a few Turks were killed and a few more made prisoners; but the rest fled and disappeared into the night, leaving piles of saddlery, ammunition, and food behind them. But the last train had left Mushaidie, and with it vanished our hopes of captured guns and prisoners. However, we had achieved the task allotted to us, and the moment the necessary pickets had been posted the rest of us forgot exhaustion, forgot victory, in the most profound sleep.

We had achieved our task, and, as the corps commander wrote, we had made the 14th of March a red-letter day for all time in the history of the regiment. I have told the story of these thirty hours of continuous marching and fighting from the point of view of a regimental officer. This is in battle, some say always, very limited in outlook. But certain things are shown clear. Waste of energy brings waste of life and victory thrown away. A regimental leader has, with his many other burdens, to endure the intolerable toil of taking thought, and of transmitting thought without pause into action. And those who work with him are not mere figures, not only items of a unit, but are intimate friends whose lives he must devote himself to preserve, whose lives he must be ready to sacrifice as freely as his own. It is well that we neither know nor decide the issues of life and death.

There is, I think, a second meaning in the oft-quoted line of Lucretius, *Nec bene promeritis capitur, nec tangitur ira*. Our prayers are not attended to perhaps because of their very foolishness. I believe when we congratulate ourselves after a battle that we and our friends are still in the land of the living, that in some mysterious way there may be a counterpart on the other side of the veil—that there may be welcome and rejoicing also on behalf of those who have passed through the

No. 1 Company Early Morning Parade Outside Samarra.

Trenches at Samarra.

BATHING IN THE TIGRIS.

THE PIONEERS OF THE REGIMENT IN SUMMER KIT.

SAMARRA.

portals of death. Although every mother's son of us must experience a feeling of dread in stepping alone into the night that no man knows, must be filled with sorrow and move with a heavy heart when his comrades and those filled with the glory of youth and promise depart, still we can, all of us, also feel thankful for the loan of their help and strength.

Two years of war, two years of living constantly in the presence of death, has brought to me, as it has brought to many, the assurance that it is well equally with those who remain here as it surely is with those who pass away. And we have no other answer to the last question ever asked by Cleek Smith. "It is only after the sun hath set that the owls of Athenae wing their flight."

The following day the battalion remained at Mushaidie; a dust storm was blowing and many reports came in of the enemy returning to make a counter-attack. But his defeat had been too severe and he made no real resistance again till we encountered him a month or so later some 30 miles further north near Istabulat. Meanwhile our brigade received orders to concentrate on the Tigris at the Babi Bend, some six miles east of Mushaidie. A pleasant week of comparative rest was spent there and then, there being no signs of the enemy, we were withdrawn to our old camping ground in the palm groves, that line the river bank between Kazimain and the City of Baghdad. The re-organisation of our platoons after the recent losses was completed, and fresh equipment and clothing issued. Two companies were split up on outpost duty, but even so time was found for military training and for some visits to the city, an equal pleasure to officers and men. The colonel was sent for to Army Headquarters, and General Maude was most complimentary to the regiment for their great fight.

In April the division moved forward, and the brigade again marched past the Babi Bend, northward of Mushaidie to Beled Station, where we had a few days' halt and some of us shot a number of sandgrouse. Thence we pressed on till we overtook the Turks entrenched beyond the Median Wall, holding a strong position about Istabulat. From this it was necessary to drive them, our objective being the railhead at Samarrah.

TENT PITCHING.

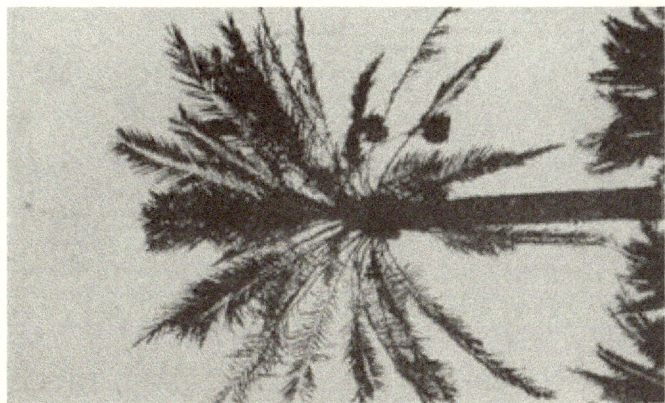

THE CULTIVATION OF THE DATE PALM AT BASRAH.

CHAPTER 8

The Battle That Won Samarrah

The following article by Brigadier-General A. G. Wauchope, C.M.G.,
D.S.O., is here republished with permission:

There stretches, some sixty miles north of Baghdad, from the Tigris to the Euphrates, a famous fortified line known to the Greeks as the Median Wall. It is skilfully constructed in tiers of mud bricks to a height fully thirty feet above the level of the plain, the whole has been covered over by a thick layer of earth protecting the bricks these many centuries from wind and weather, for the Median Wall is, so some say, the oldest building in all the world. It formed certainly the outer line of the defences of the Kingdom of Babylon under Nebuchadnezzar II, when it ran from Opis on the Tigris to Hit on the Euphrates and this line in far earlier times marked the boundary between the two ancient peoples of Akkad and Sumer, and was probably even then a fortification of first importance.

However that may be, it stands to-day the most prominent landmark in all this district of the Tigris valley; though broken, tumbledown mounds represent the great wall towards the Euphrates, for many miles near the Tigris it stands without a break, with strong projecting bastions to give flank defence every forty or fifty yards, and at wider intervals the wall rises so as to form some sort of keep or watch tower.

Whoever built the great wall built it for the purposes of war, and no building, I venture to say, has ever had so many battles fought within its neighbourhood. Every race through every age, Aryan and Turanian, Babylonian and Assyrian, Median and Persian, armies from Greece and armies from Rome, have, during the past thousands of years, slaughtered each other with extraordinary thoroughness below these mud bastions; and more recently, but with the same seeming

Date Palm Scenes below Basrah.

T. Henderson. M.C. G.V. Stewart. C. Ryrie.

At Arab Village.

Undepressed.

futility, Turk has murdered Arab and Arab Turk, the destruction of villages, mosques and canals marking, as of old, the soldiers sacrifice to the God of War.

Standing this morning on these ancient ramparts, I watch the sun rise over this land which, once so rich and fertile, now shows hardly a sign of human habitation, this country where not a tree nor a house has been allowed for many years to stand, over which the blight of misrule has lain as a curse for centuries and I see yet one more army going forth to battle; once again columns of armed men sweep forth to encounter similar columns, to kill and to capture within sight of the Median Wall. And watching these columns of Englishmen and Highlanders, of Hindus, Gurkhas and bearded Sikhs advancing to the coming conflict, one felt the conviction that this struggle was being fought for the sake of principles more lofty, for ends more permanent, for aims less fugitive, for issues of higher service to the cause of humanity, than those that had animated the innumerable and bloody conflicts of the past.

The delta of the Tigris ends a few miles below Samarrah. That is to say, whoever holds the district about Samarrah controls the waters of the Tigris. For lower down in the Baghdad *valaiyet* the river in its annual flood deposits so much mud on its bed as to raise itself in course of centuries, above the level of the plain. Consequently, artificial banks about three feet high have been built all along the river, and were these to be cut during the flood season, the whole surrounding country would be inundated and the spring crops destroyed. This renders the districts of Samarrah of great natural importance, and the fact that the Germans had completed a railway between Baghdad and Samarrah, made it also desirable for the British to hold it.

The country here differs little from the rest of the Tigris valley, the same level plain of loam and mud, a strip of two or three miles nearest the river highly irrigated, and at this season, green with young corn and barley; further afield the bare, brown, featureless desert stretching out endlessly in every direction. Dawn and dusk transform this shadowless wilderness into a land of the most wonderful colour and atmosphere, but throughout the heat of the day the glare and dust make it hateful to white men. And even in April, the shade temperature runs to 110 degrees Fahrenheit, and where troops march in this country without trees there is no shade from the sun, no escape from the heat.

Besides the Median Wall, there remain two outward and visible

157

THE ARCH OF CTESIPHON.

THE REGIMENT PASSING THE ARCH OF CTESIPHON *EN ROUTE* FOR BAGHDAD, MARCH 1917.

The Entrance to the Mosque Kadhimain.

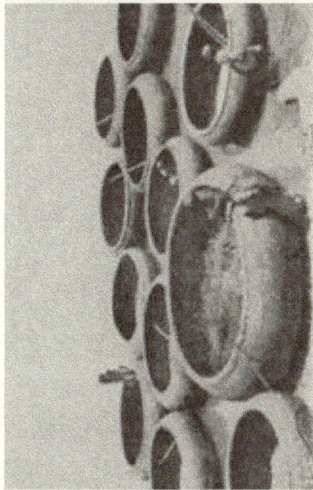

"Gufas" or Circular Boats at Baghdad.

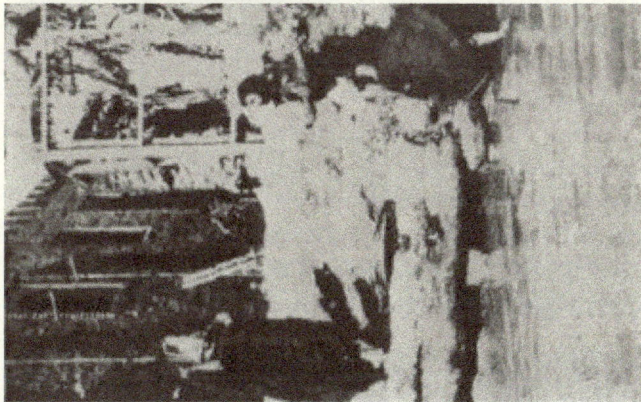

Women drawing water from the river.

signs of the older civilisation that flourished in happier times. There are, at frequent intervals, low flat mounds composed of old sunbaked bricks the sites of ancient cities; so numerous are these that they seem to justify the Chaldean proverb, boasting of the prosperity of the people, that a cock may spring from house to house without lighting on the ground from Babylon to the sea.

The other are the walls of the canals that served to irrigate the country between the two rivers. These canals have for centuries past been dry and useless, but their walls, twenty or thirty feet high, and many miles in length, remain as the most conspicuous monument of the fallen greatness of Mesopotamia. That they will again be put to their original purpose was the confident assertion of Sir William Willcocks, and with Turkish misrule finally banished from the land, a few years may see these canals again filled with water, bringing wealth and plenty to a happier generation. But today they seem to have but the one use of acting as tactical features on the battlefield, as was indeed the case in this fight near Istabulat.

For some days before the 31st April, the British had been collecting behind the Median Wall, facing the Turkish position which lay some three miles to the north of the Wall, and some twelve miles south of Samarrah.

A very well selected position it proved, and a very difficult one to attack. The Turkish left rested securely on a re-entrant bend of the Tigris. Thence the line ran east and west across the Dujail River, and continued for a mile along a dry canal, until it met the railway a little to the north of Istabulat station. Both the Railway and the Dujail run roughly north-west to south-east, but the Tigris towards Samarrah bends due west. Consequently the Turks by refusing their right were able to rest that flank on the ruins of the ancient city of Istabulat. These ruins consisted of some low mounds and the high walls of an old canal that had run from the Tigris across the present line of the Railway four miles to the north of the station. The whole country was absolutely flat and bare, except for the broken and uneven walls of the Dujail River and Istabulat Canal.

The so-called Dujail River is a canal that takes off from the right bank of the Tigris some four miles north of the Median Wall. It has been dug and re-dug, till it now flows below the level of the surrounding country, but its walls are fully twenty feet high, and so form the one dominant tactical feature of the level Tigris plain in this district. A couple of miles south of Istabulat station, the Dujail cuts through the Median Wall about a mile to the east of the Railway, which runs from Baghdad through the Median Wall, past Istabulat, and so on to Samarrah.

By the 18th April, the British were holding that part of the Median Wall that runs roughly for a couple of miles eastwards from the Dujail River to the River Tigris, other troops, also in rear of the Median Wall, continued our line on the west bank of the Dujail, and a third body was held in reserve. The open nature of the country, and the difficulty of distinguishing the enemy's main position from his advanced trenches, made the problem of attack uncommonly difficult, and the thorough bombardment of his trenches before assault almost impossible.

The key to the position was obviously the high double wall of the Dujail River. These walls are a hundred to a hundred and fifty yards wide at the top, and being very broken and uneven give some cover to skirmishers in attack or defence. An attack along this line is also made somewhat easier by a small ridge of sandhills that had originally formed the walls of an old canal, which flowed in earlier centuries between the Tigris and the Dujail. Photographs taken by our airmen showed that the Turks had strengthened their line where it crossed the Dujail, by building a strong redoubt on its eastern bank some 300 yards long by 150 broad; here too were a number of machine gun emplacements and, a little in rear, six or eight gun pits.

On the 18th a Highland Regiment pushed forward a strong patrol along the east bank of the Dujail, an Indian Battalion doing the same on the west bank, the two patrols working together and giving each other mutual support. Both Regiments encountered the Turkish outposts within six hundred yards, and after driving them some distance back, the patrols were withdrawn at night.

As an attack on the enemy position was decided on, the battalion commander suggested that a line of strong points should be constructed about a mile ahead of our line, that when these had been made good, a second line of strong points a further eight hundred yards in advance should be constructed, so that by this means the final assault might be made from a short distance to the enemy's main position, and also by this means artillery officers would be able to locate definitely the enemy's main trenches and the guns could be brought up within 2,000 yards before the Infantry should assault. This idea was adopted.

During the 19th the Highland Regiment, by some fine patrol

work, drove the enemy advanced troops back with little loss, and during the night three strong points were built a mile in advance, two on the east and one on the west bank of the Dujail. From these points both the Highlanders and the Punjabis skirmished further forward on the 20th, and the enemy's position was becoming seriously threatened with but little loss to ourselves.

One incident in this patrol fighting must not pass unnoted. An artillery officer had been sent forward in the morning to observe the ground and enemy positions from our strong point on the east bank of the Dujail. It was a task of considerable danger, for already several of our men had been hit by enemy snipers, and at this moment a wounded man was being carried back by the stretcher bearers. The artillery officer had crawled a little ahead of the Strong Point in order to observe more freely, but his gallantry was ill rewarded by a bullet striking him and incapacitating him from coming back, or even escaping from his exposed position.

Easton had been sergeant of the Highlanders stretcher bearers since his predecessor had been killed when recovering wounded, and he himself had won the Distinguished Conduct Medal for a fine piece of work in France. Without hesitation Easton now ran forward from the strong point and, though the enemy snipers were dropping bullets all round, roughly bandaged the officer, picked him up on his back, staggered down to the river and got him across under the welcome shelter of the other bank, though the stream was over six feet deep. For this action Sergeant Easton now wears a bar to his Distinguished Conduct Medal.

On the 20th it was definitely decided that the situation demanded an immediate advance, and a direct frontal attack was ordered to take place at dawn on the following morning. One force were to lead the attack at 5 a.m. on the east of the Dujail, the Highlanders to advance along the east bank of that canal, and one Company of the Punjabis on the west bank. On the right of the Highlanders a battalion of Gurkhas were to advance from the right strong point with a battalion of Indian Infantry in echelon on their right near the Tigris, another battalion being held in reserve. When this attack had gained ground a second force was to advance over the bare plain on the west of the Dujail, and their right to gain touch with the left of the Company of Punjabis on the Dujail bank. The objectives of the main attack were the redoubt, and the two bridges which crossed the Dujail immediately above it. A third force was held back in reserve.

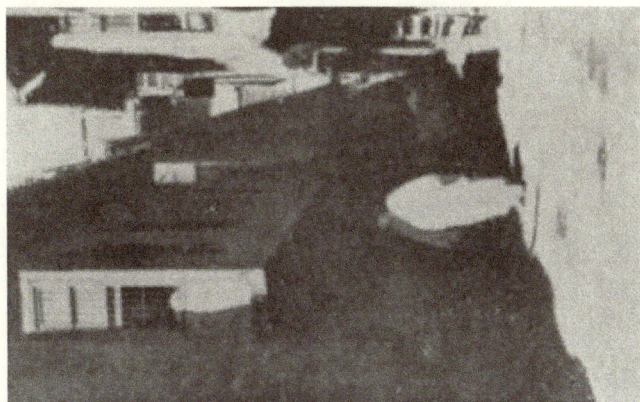

Street Scenes in Baghdad.

BRITISH RESIDENCY, BAGHDAD.

HOTEL MAUDE, BAGHDAD.

THE BRIDGE AT BAGHDAD.

The orders were thus very clear, and the plan simple; the main difficulty was to ensure effective artillery co-operation, since to come within effective range of the redoubt our batteries would be forced to move forward over very open ground, and counter-battery work would be obviously hard to arrange.

The frontage of broken ground open to the Highlanders was but little over 150 yards; the commanding officer therefore wisely determined to attack on a narrow frontage of two platoons rather than expose his men on the bare plain, and with the Dujail giving the direction to his left, trust to the impetus of eight lines to force the enemy's position.

Precisely at 5 a.m., the covering batteries opened fire on the enemy outposts, the leading platoons charged forward and, without pausing to fire, but advancing by a series of swift rushes drove back the Turkish advanced troops about a thousand yards from our strong points. A few Turks were bayoneted, a number more shot by the fire of a well-placed Lewis gun, but the surprise of the attack and the rapidity of its execution saved our men from any severe loss during this first advance. But as our leading platoons drew near to the enemy main positions, they came under an enfilade fire from the west bank of the Dujail, and a number of men had to swing round to the left, and, from the crest of the wall, reply to the enemy not two hundred yards distant on the opposite bank.

The succeeding lines, however, pressed forward, section after section rushed on to the help of their comrades, every rise and every knoll along the river was held by snipers and the battle developed into a fierce contest between skirmishers. But it was not of long duration. Shortly after 6 o'clock nearly two miles of country had been cleared of the enemy, our men were not to be denied, and the leading section of Highlanders made a gallant charge and rushed the main redoubt, killing a certain number of its defenders and driving out the remainder. The success of the attack was greatly due to the rapidity, but its very rapidity had led to considerable intervals occurring between the eight lines that had originally advanced to the assault.

Some platoons had been forced to engage the enemy on the opposite bank, others with Lewis guns were keeping down the fire of the enemy who were holding several small trenches ahead, and a number of men had fallen, never to rise again; consequently for the first few minutes there were less than a hundred men in the redoubt, and these were subject to a heavy fire from their front, and enfilading fire from their left.

Now was the moment when artillery support was most needed. But as before explained, this, owing to the nature of the ground, had been most difficult to arrange. The batteries posted under cover of the Median Wall, soon found themselves, as the enemy retired, at extreme range, had been obliged in consequence to advance to new positions. This is a matter which takes longer than the actual bringing up of the guns; fresh observations must be made by artillery officers, new telephone wires must be made, new communications established, and correct ranges ascertained of the new targets before effective support can be given. This was all being done, but under great difficulties, because the enemy had established a strong barrage in rear of the assaulting troops. Many of our gunners were hit, especially among the telephone operators; consequently, just at this critical time, there was little or no artillery support to be had.

Now the Turk is a stubborn fighter. His men on the west bank of the Dujail had not yet been driven so far back as those opposing the Highlanders, and they now opened a very galling fire from the west bank at a range of only two to four hundred yards. The redoubt had been taken at 6-15 a.m. Within ten minutes the Turks on the east bank had organised a strong body to make a counter attack, and these headed by parties of bombers, rushed the redoubt, drove the few defenders back, and held its front and side faces. But their triumph was short lived. It was a proud boast of the Highlanders that of all the miles of entrenchments that had at one time or another been entrusted to them not one yard had even been surrendered to the enemy; it was their stern resolve that no Highlander should lie unavenged, that no man who wore the Red Haeckle should give his life in vain.

The redoubt had once been theirs, and in its trenches lay the bodies of their comrades who had died to hold it. It was the redoubt they had set forth to capture; now more than ever they were determined that not a live Turk should dispute possession. The platoons that had originally formed the rear waves were now fast coming up, bombs and bombers were called for, and an immediate counter-attack organised. But the losses were now very heavy. Within a minute, one captain and two subalterns were killed, two captains and two subalterns wounded, and a heavy proportion among the rank and file also fell. The smallest hesitation, the slightest wavering, and the Turks had made good their success. But there was no hesitation and, though only one unwounded officer remained, there was no wavering. The bombers dashed for-

167

The Quartermaster, Assistant Adjutant, Transport Officer,
2nd in Command, and the Colonel watching
the Regimental Sports at the Front.

The Mesopotamian Railway.

CAPTAIN T. W. STEWART, CAPTAIN W. A. YOUNG AND THE PADRE.

ward, every available man followed, and within fifteen minutes of its loss, the entire redoubt was recaptured and its forward trenches rapidly consolidated. The Highlanders' boast still held true, the Red Haeckle was again victorious.

Many were the dead, many the wounded to testify to the gallant deeds that led to this success. An artillery officer, who witnessed the assault, wrote:—

> That day the Highlanders without help won a victory that only those who saw it can realise was among the most gallant fought in this war.

What is the secret, whence comes this spirit, of the wave of bravery that seizes soldiers at these great moments? Many of the very men who charged forward had, but ten minutes before, been driven back, many of their comrades lay dead beside them, they had lost their accustomed leaders, shrapnel and heavy shell were bursting among them, and when the cry for bombs and bombers was given, it must have seemed to many to be but the prelude to disaster, the vain cry for further and useless sacrifice. What is it then that stops the individual from hanging back, from letting others lead, from justifying himself to himself by continuing to fire in comparative safety at longer ranges? Who would detect him? Might he not argue plausibly enough, that his covering fire would be of more assistance to his comrades than his rushing uselessly forward at their head? The secret of it lies in *esprit de corps*, in the willing surrender by the individual of his freedom of action, by the voluntary sacrifice of the individual for the good of all. *And greater love hath no man than this:—that he giveth his life for his friend.*

The gallantry of those who lie dead, whether British, or Indian, or Turk cannot be told, but one incident that was witnessed by several is worthy of record. The redoubt measured several hundred yards on its front and side faces, and the attackers were few in number. One of these, Private Melvin had by some chance so damaged his bayonet that he could not fix it on his rifle. Throwing that weapon aside, he rushed forward where his comrades were scarce, and the enemy in plenty, and encountered a group of Turks single handed. With bayonet and fist he brought three to the ground, the remaining six, stunned by the violence of his attack, surrendered, and were brought back by this brave old soldier in triumph to his company. For this deed Private Melvin was subsequently awarded the Victoria Cross.

The Colonel.

The Adjutant.

THE MOSQUES OF BAGHDAD.

Battalion Headquarters now moved up close in rear of the redoubt, the telephonic communication was established with the brigade, and companies reorganised according to their losses. And fortunate it was that this was done with no loss of time. For the Turk had intended to hold this line of entrenchments, of which the redoubt was the key, and the main defence of the two bridges, throughout the summer, and he was not going to surrender the position without further struggle. Two counter-attacks formed up and advanced against the front face of the redoubt, a few Turks got within fifty or a hundred yards of the redoubt, but each attack was broken up by steady rifle fire and Lewis gun fire, and our position made more secure.

A little *nullah* ran from the Turks' second position to within fifty yards of the redoubt, and up this channel from time to time he sent parties of bombers, but these were easily held in check. A group of machine guns from further up the Dujail swept the crest of the hard-won parapet, and men less experienced in war had suffered more than did those who bore the Red Haeckle. But no experience of war could save men from the high explosive shell which burst throughout the day among the trenches, destroying indiscriminately parapet and defenders. These 5.9 shell the Highlanders had known all too well in France, and the number of bursts reminded our men rather of a bombardment in the trenches of Flanders than the shell fire ordinary to Mesopotamia. And to this bombardment the defenders of the redoubt were subject from time to time throughout that long day.

It is a constant puzzle, why in this life so many things that are at first merely disagreeable are allowed to make so great a noise and to continue for so long a time that they become almost unbearable. It is a question that often confronts one at a comic opera, always in the near neighbourhood of a gramophone, but never with such persistent irritation as when undergoing a bombardment from high explosive shell. Nothing is more trying to the nerves, for and from it there is no escape. This war has been defined as a war, not of infantry, nor of artillery, but of effective co-operation between the two.

The nature of the ground, and the skill with which the enemy had chosen his positions had prevented this co-operation from being as effective as is usual in our army, and this in spite of every effort being made by our artillery officers, and in spite of many casualties among their batteries. In consequence, the enemy's batteries were never silenced, and kept up a heavy fire throughout the day, and our losses were heavy. On our right the Gurkhas had advanced in gallant style at

SAMARRA.

WIRELESS STATION,
BAGHDAD. DESTROYED
BY THE HUNS.

SAMARRA RAILWAY STATION.

Resting after the Battle of Istabulat.

No. 4 Company before Istabulat under The Median Wall. P. Smyth, A. E. Baristow, R. Walker, and G.V. Stewart in Foreground.

Ground over which the Regiment advanced to attack the Turkish strong point beneath the +.

the same time as the Highlanders, and in spite of a stubborn resistance had pushed the enemy back along the line of the old canal, and kept up with our advance.

Then with the sand dunes dipped to the level of the plain and the salient bend of the Tigris narrowed their front, the Gurkhas swung round to their left in a most soldierly fashion, and, despite, heavy losses, joined the Highlanders on the Dujail, and for the rest of the day shared the honours and the dangers of the defence of the redoubt and the trenches near it. The Indian regiment advancing still further on the right had met with misfortune, for, on reaching a small rise in the ground, their lines had been suddenly swept with machine gun fire at a range of three hundred yards. Many men fell within the space of a few minutes, and it became necessary to bring up the reserve battalion to their assistance.

Consequently no further advance was possible on this flank, nor on the west flank did the situation offer any greater promise. The Punjabi Regiment on the immediate left of the Highlanders had fought under great difficulties, but with such determination that they eventually dug themselves in opposite the Redoubt on the west bank of the Dujail, though half their men were killed or wounded. On their left again, another Highland Battalion, old friends of ours, both in peace and war, had pressed the enemy back, and occupied some eight hundred yards of an old irrigation channel that ran westward from the Dujail towards the railway. Further to the west, this dry channel remained in the hands of the Turks, and bombing attacks were carried on throughout the day. Another battalion had also suffered considerably from shell fire, and was posted in echelon on the left rear.

It was evident that without a renewed bombardment and strong reinforcements, no further advance was possible on either side. We had advanced a couple of miles, driven the enemy from his strongest positions, and gained our immediate objectives. It was evident, that to the day following must be left the final advance and capture of Samarrah.

This account of the fighting near Samarrah purports to give no general view of the whole action. Enough, if something clear is shown of the part played by one regiment, and of the fighting by its immediate neighbours. The Highlanders had had some tough battles during the past few months, and during this day's fighting had lost over a third of their total strength in killed and wounded.

On the next morning it was found that the Turks had retired several miles on to the ruins of the ancient city of Istabulat, but it was not until the afternoon that the battle was continued. Then it was fought with the same violence, and with equal stubbornness as on the day before. Again the Turk was driven out of his positions, and again, like the gallant fighter he is, he held on till nightfall.

Orders were given to renew the attack at dawn on the third day of the battle, but as day broke the patrols of Highlanders sent back word that the enemy had evacuated his forward positions, and we advanced in attack formation straight on Samarrah. The Highlanders were leading, and passed through the ancient ruins and the several lines of enemy trenches; those trenches held so stubbornly by the Turk, empty now, save for groups of dead bodies and a few of unhappy wounded who had not been moved during the night. Surely the world offers no scene more pitiful than that of a battlefield after action.

I know, by personal experience, the suffering entailed in lying day and night untended with broken limbs, the utter weariness from wounds, and the exhaustion after conflict, the tragedy of all surroundings, the cries of those who cry for help that never comes, a passionate longing for death alternating with a craven fear of foe and wandering marauder, and above all, the horror of the great vultures swinging round and round in ever closer circles. Little of the pomp or ceremony of war was seen by the Highlanders as they marched that morning through the Turkish entrenchments at the head of the British troops, the first regiment to enter Samarrah as they had marched some six weeks earlier the first to enter Baghdad.

Such is the story of the part played by the Highland Regiment in this hard-fought battle, but though I have told the tale from the point of view of a regimental officer, I am not forgetful of the deeds of others. My endeavour has been to give a picture of events as one man meets them in a course of a day's fighting, not to give a narrative of deeds of which I know little and saw nothing. But of the gallant help given by the Gurkhas I have spoken and, after some experience of war both in France and in Mesopotamia, I add my testimony to the value of the loyal services rendered by so many of our Indian regiments; it will stand to their honour for all time that they have fought throughout these years so bravely and so faithfully. War is a noble comradeship, and the ties that now bind the Indian and British troops will not easily be severed.

The relationship between British and Indian officers is invariably happy; difficulties of language, however, sometimes give a little humour to a long campaign. When I was first given command of a brigade formed of both British and Indian battalions I made a point of speaking to each Indian officer, and saying something in appreciation of his services. To this the senior Indian officer replied with the usual Eastern compliments, and then added:—

Many Generals have come to see us, but each usually spares us but a couple of minutes; you, in your kindness, have spoken to each of us for half an hour and we shall indeed fight bravely for you, for of all Generals, you, O Brigadier, are the most long minded.

AT THE FRONT. THE REGIMENT IN THE SAN-I-YAT TRENCHES. SER-GEANT BISSET AND SERGEANT MURDOCH BOTH KILLED IN ACTION.

THAT ABLE ADMINISTRATOR GENERAL SIR PERCY L. COX
AND AN INFLUENTIAL ARAB SHEIKH.

CHAPTER 9

Rolls and Orders

On April 20th, Colonel J. Stewart took over the command of the regiment, and Colonel A. G. Wauchope became a brigadier.

It was a great blow to the regiment to lose their colonel, and very difficult for any other man coming after him; but the new colonel proved a worthy successor to the old and the regiment was fortunate in having two such men in succession to guard its interests and its honour. Months later when I congratulated the general on the successes of his old regiment and on his promotion, he said, "Yes, yes, B., the regiment was splendid, but I am not too sure that the other matter is altogether a matter for congratulation." I felt certain that had it been left to his own choice he would have preferred to remain with his Highlanders than accept any higher command.

With the capture of Samarrah it can be said that the winter campaign of 1916-1917 came to an end. We held the rail head of the Baghdad railway and had captured sixteen locomotives, 224 trucks and two barges of ammunition. Already at the end of April, the heat of the coming summer which was to prove the hottest on record could be felt, and the thermometer in that month reached 114° in the shade.

The actual fighting was for the time being practically over, and it was decided that Samarrah should be our advanced position on the Tigris. Preparations were at once commenced to make the position a strong one, and sufficient to hold up any attack which the enemy might have in view; but the summer coming on the Turks were not anxious to be aggressive and took up their most advanced positions some five or six miles further up the Tigris.

The summer was consequently passed under much more pleasant conditions than in 1916. The Turks being far distant a number of officers and men were granted a month's leave to India; tents, rations and comforts were plentiful. The regiment was at full strength and, despite the heat, the men maintained their health throughout the summer. The main task was the digging of several lines of trenches in front of the old city of Samarrah, but training was carried on continuously so that the regiment might be ready as always for whatever operations were to take place in the coming cold weather.

The battalion had now spent nearly two years in Mesopotamia, and of the thousand who landed not two hundred remained, and of these many had been wounded. What contrasts the two years offer. In the first period one effort succeeded another, but neither training nor valour were sufficient to redress the balance of the scales, and despite every sacrifice Kut fell. Then came the months when we held San-i-yat, when there were few men and arduous duties, intolerable heat and no comfort.

The spring of the second year was marked by a succession of victories, and achievements for all time memorable; the forcing of San-i-yat, the entry to Baghdad, the battles of Mushaidie and Istabulat; and finally the last few months of comparative peace and plenty.

Throughout the two years the indomitable spirit of the battalion showed itself true to the finest traditions of the regiment, and it is open to question whether memory of the hundred survivors fighting their way back from the Turkish trenches on the 21st of January, does not extort as much admiration as the memory of the three companies, after 30 hours of continuous marching and successful fighting, charging at midnight into the station at Mushaidie.

SUMMARY OF OFFICER CASUALTIES
suffered by the 2nd Bn. during its service in Mesopotamia,
July 1916 to May 1917.

Killed in Action	16	Includes Captain Duncan, R.A.M.C., and 2/Lieut. A. E. Sinclair.
Died from wounds	8	...
Died from disease	1	...
Missing	2	Captain D. C. Hamilton Johnstone and 2/Lieut. H. F. Forrester. Both wounded.
Prisoners of War	1	2/Lieut. A. H. Quine.
Wounded in Action	42	Includes officers wounded more than once, each occasion being counted separately. Does not include cases where officers have subsequently died from wounds.
Invalided to India	50	As above, includes instances of invaliding more than one as separate items. Also includes all cases of officers wounded who were in consequence thereof invalided.

DETAILS OF OFFICER CASUALTIES
in important battles.

	Killed in action.	Died from wounds.	Wounded.	Missing	P. of W.
7th January, 1916	3	..	16	..	..
21st January, 1916	2	..	3	1	..
22nd April, 1916	5	..	2	1	..
14th March, 1917	1	4	5	..	..
21st April, 1917	2	3	4	..	1
TOTAL	13	7	30	2	1

LIST OF OFFICERS WHO SERVED WITH THE 2ND BATTALION IN MESOPOTAMIA, 1916-17.

Brig.-General A. G. Wauchope, C.M.G., D.S.O.
Embarked, Marseilles, 5th December, 1915.
Disembarked, Basrah, 31st December, 1915.
Wounded in Action, 7th January, 1916.
Invalided to India, 16th January, 1916.
Re-embarked, Bombay, 9th May, 1916.
Disembarked, Basrah, 18th May, 1916.
To be Bt.-Lt.-Colonel, 2nd June, 1916.
Promotion to rank of Major ante-dated to 15th September 1914.
(*London Gaz.*, dated 14th September, 1916).
To be Bt.-Colonel, 23rd December, 1916.
Assumed Command, Brigade. 20th April, 1917.
To be Bde. Commander, 11th May, 1917.

Colonel J. Stewart.
Embarked, Devonport, 26th December, 1916.
Disembarked, Basrah, 21st March, 1917.
To be A.-Lt.-Col. whilst Commanding a Battn. 5th May, 1917.

Major T. G. F. Cochrane.
Embarked, Marseilles, 5th December, 1915.
Disembarked, Basrah, 31st December, 1915.
Wounded in Action, 7th January, 1916.
Invalided to India, 16th January, 1916.
Re-embarked, Bombay, 27th August, 1916.
Disembarked, Basrah, 2nd September, 1916.

To be A/Major whilst 2nd in Command, 14th September, 1916.
Relinquishes above, 15th April, 1917.
To be A/Major on H. Q. of a Battn., 15th May, 1917.

Major D. C. Hamilton-Johnstone.
Embarked, Marseilles, 5th December, 1915.
Disembarked, Basrah, 31st December, 1915.
To be Tempy. Major, 7th January, 1916.
Wounded and Missing, 21st-22nd January, 1916.

Major C. R. B. Henderson.
Embarked, Marseilles, 26th December, 1915.
Disembarked, Basrah, 26th January, 1916.
Promoted Major, 8th January, 1916.
Invalided to India, 14th April, 1916.
Tenure of Adjt. expired, 4th January, 1917.

Major The Rev. Andrew Macfarlane.
Embarked, Marseilles, 5th December, 1915.
Disembarked, Basrah, 31st December, 1915.

Major The Hon. R. T. C. Murray.
Embarked, Devonport, 10th February, 1916.
Disembarked, Basrah, 14th March, 1916.
To India for duty with A. H. Q., 3rd April, 1916.

Captain J. Anderson.
Embarked, Marseilles, 5th December, 1915.
Disembarked, Basrah, 31st December, 1915.
To be Hony. Captain, 3rd June, 1916.

Captain J. A. Barstow,
M.C. Embarked, Devonport, 11th July, 1916.
Disembarked, Basrah, 10th August, 1916.
Wounded in Action, 21st April, 1917.

Captain A. E. Blair.
Embarked, Devonport, 10th February, 1916.
Disembarked, Basrah, 14th March, 1916.

Captain H. John Blampied.
Embarked, Devonport, 7th June, 1916.
Disembarked, Basrah, 4th July, 1916.
To be Asst. Censor, 28th January, 1917.
To be Censor, I.E.F. "D", 1st April, 1917.

Captain R. H. Crake (Attached).
Held command of Btn. during latter portion of January, 1916.

Captain P. G. Egerton.
Posted to the Battalion, 30th June, 1917.

Captain C. D. Gilmour, M.C.
Embarked, Devonport, 20th January, 1916.
Disembarked, Basrah, 21st February, 1916.
Wounded in Action, 22nd April, 1916.
Invalided to India, 2nd May, 1916. To England, 11th June, 1916.
Awarded the Military Cross, 22nd December, 1916.

Captain A. M. Grieve.
Embarked, Devonport, 16th February, 1916.
Disembarked, Basrah, 23rd March, 1916.
Invalided to India, 5th July, 1916.
Re-embarked, Bombay, 27th May, 1917.
Disembarked, Basrah, 4th June, 1917.

Captain J. B. S. Haldane.
Embarked, Devonport, 9th October, 1916.
Disembarked, Basrah, 2nd December, 1916.
Wounded in Action, 22nd February, 1917.
Invalided to India, 19th March, 1917.

Captain J. N. Inglis.
Embarked, Devonport, 20th January, 1916.
Disembarked, Basrah, 21st February, 1916.
Killed in Action, 22nd April, 1916.

Captain R. Macfarlane, M.C.
Embarked, Bombay, 11th April, 1916.
Disembarked Basrah, 17th April, 1916.
(Date of Embarkation in U. K. is not known).
Wounded in Action, 10th June, 1916.
Camp Area Comdt., Ma'gil, 14th July, 1916.
Wounded in Action, 14th March, 1917.
Awarded the Military Cross, 31st March, 1917.
Killed in Action, 21st April, 1917.

Captain M. E. Park, D.S.O.
Embarked, Marseilles, 25th November, 1915.
Disembarked, Basrah, 28th December, 1915.
Wounded in Action, 7th January, 1916.

Wounded in Action, 10th April, 1916.
Awarded the Silver Medal for Valour by H. M. the King of Italy.

Captain R. M. Purvis.
Embarked, Marseilles, 5th December, 1915.
Disembarked, Basrah, 31st December, 1915.
Wounded in Action, 7th January, 1916.
Invalided to India, 20th January, 1916.
Re-embarked, Bombay, 17th March, 1916.
Disembarked, Basrah, 24th March, 1916.
Wounded in Action, 10th April, 1916.
Invalided to India, 27th April, 1916.
Re-embarked, Bombay, 20th January, 1917.
Disembarked, Basrah, 28th January, 1917.
Died from wounds, 14th March, 1917.
Promoted Captain, from 8th March, 1916.
(*London Gaz.*, dated 23rd August, 1916.)

Captain R. D. Robertson.
Posted, December, 1917.

Captain N. M. Ritchie, D.S.O.
Embarked, Devonport, 20th January, 1916.
Disembarked, Basrah, 21st February, 1916.
To be Adjutant, *vice* Major C. R. B. Henderson, 5th January, 1917.
Invalided to India, 12th June, 1917.
Awarded the D.S.O., 1917.

Captain K. W. L. Simonet (Attached).
Posted for temporary duty, 16th January, 1916.
Killed in Action, 21st January, 1916.

Captain J. Todd.
Embarked, Marseilles, 10th December, 1915.
Disembarked, Basrah, 13th January, 1916.
Apptd. Transport Officer, 22nd July, 1916.

Captain L. H. Willett.
Embarked, Devonport, 9th October, 1916.
Disembarked, Basrah, 2nd December, 1916.
Wounded in Action, 21st April, 1917.
Invalided to India, 8th May, 1917.

Captain W. A. Young, M. C.
Embarked, Marseilles, 5th December, 1915.

Disembarked, Basrah, 31st December, 1915.
Wounded in Action, 7th January, 1916.
Invalided to India, 20th January, 1916.
Re-embarked, Bombay, 17th March, 1916.
Disembarked, Basrah, 24th March, 1916.
To be T/Lieut., Supmy., 8th July, 1916.
Wounded in Action, 22nd February, 1917.
Awarded the Military Cross.

Captain The Rev. A. Silver.
Posted to the Regiment, 30th April, 1917.

Captain A. W. Duncan, R.A.M.C.
Embarked, Marseilles, 5th December, 1915.
Disembarked, Basrah, 31st December, 1915.
Was killed in Action whilst M. O. with another Regiment,
9th March, 1916.

Captain G. F. Gunlette, R.A.M.C.
For duty as M. O., 24th March, 1917.
Relieved, 28th March, 1917.

Captain J. Macqueen, R.A.M.C.
Joined Bn. as M. O., 18th July, 1916.
Struck off, tour expired, 25th March, 1917.

Captain W. Moore Cameron, R.A.M.C.
Posted as M. O., 28th March, 1917.

Captain T. W. Stewart.
Embarked, Devonport, 24th May, 1916.
Disembarked, Basrah, 13th June, 1916.
Invalided to India, 31st January, 1917.

LIEUTENANTS.

H. Bowie.
Embarked, Marseilles, 5th December, 1915.
Disembarked, Basrah, 31st December, 1915.
Wounded in Action, 7th January, 1916.
Invalided to India, 16th January, 1916.
Relinquishes Tempy. rank of Lieutenant, 7th January, 1916.

W. Coutts Hunter.
Embarked, Marseilles, 5th December, 1915.
Disembarked, Basrah, 31st December, 1915.
Wounded in Action, 7th January, 1916.

Invalided to India, 20th January, 1916.
To England from Egypt, 19th March, 1916.

C. V. S. Cooks.
Embarked, Marseilles, 5th December, 1915.
Disembarked, Basrah, 31st December, 1915.
Wounded in Action, 7th January, 1916.
Invalided to India, 16th January, 1916.
Invalided to England, 7th April, 1916.

G. Curdie.
Embarked, Marseilles, 5th December, 1915.
Disembarked, Basrah, 31st December, 1915.
Wounded in Action, 21st January, 1916.
Invalided to India, 4th February, 1916.
Promoted T/Capt., 23rd November, 1915.
Relinquishes Tempy. rank, 19th January, 1916.
Invalided to England, from Egypt, 7th April, 1916.

A. B. Cumming.
Embarked, Marseilles, 25th November, 1915.
Disembarked, Basrah, 28th December, 1915.
Wounded in Action, 7th January, 1916.
Invalided to India, 20th January, 1916.
Re-embarked, Bombay, 25th March, 1916.
Disembarked, Basrah, 1st April, 1916.
Killed in Action, 22nd April, 1916.

J. F. C. Dixon, M.C.
Embarked, Marseilles, 5th December, 1915.
Disembarked, Basrah, 31st December, 1915.
Wounded in Action, 7th January, 1916.
Wounded in Action, 21st January, 1916.
Invalided to India, 30th January, 1916.
Re-embarked, Bombay, 9th June, 1916.
Disembarked Basrah, 16th June, 1916.
To be Lieutenant, 18th July, 1916.
Invalided to India, 23rd November, 1916.
Awarded the Military Cross, 22nd December 1916.

R. H. Dundas.
Embarked, Marseilles, 5th December, 1915.
Disembarked, Basrah, 31st December, 1915.
Wounded in Action, 21st January, 1916.

Invalided to India, 7th March, 1916.

F. J. Fell.
Posted to Battalion, 9th December, 1917.

J. O. Hutchinson.
Embarked, Marseilles, 5th December, 1915.
Disembarked, Basrah, 31st December, 1915.
Killed in Action, 7th January, 1916.

R. W. Macfarlane Grieve.
Embarked, Marseilles, 5th December, 1915.
Disembarked, Basrah, 31st December, 1915.
Wounded in Action, 7th January, 1916.
Invalided to India, 20th January 1916.
Re-embarked, Bombay, 6th April, 1916.
Disembarked, Basrah, 13th April, 1916.
Invalided to India, 26th November, 1916.

C. J. Mcconaghey.
Embarked, Devonport, 16th February, 1916.
Disembarked, Basrah, 23rd March, 1916.
Killed in Action, 22nd April, 1916.

W. W. Mcewan, M. C.
Embarked, Marseilles, 12th December, 1915.
Disembarked, Basrah, 21st January, 1916.
To Regiment, 1st March, 1916.
Wounded in Action, 22nd April, 1916.
Invalided to India, 2nd May, 1916.
Re-embarked, Karachi, 14th August, 1916.
Disembarked, Basrah, 20th August, 1916.
Invalided to India, 30th October, 1916.
Awarded the Military Cross, 22nd December, 1916.
Re-embarked, Bombay, 17th May, 1917.
Disembarked, Basrah, 23rd May, 1917.

H. A. T. Plunkett.
Embarked, Marseilles, 5th December, 1915.
Disembarked, Basrah, 31st December, 1915.
Killed in Action, 7th January, 1916.

G. G. B. Miller Stirling.
Embarked, Suez, 21st June, 1916.
Disembarked, Basrah, 4th July, 1916.

Died from Wounds, 14th March, 1917.

D. C. Stewart Smith.
Embarked, Marseilles, 5th December, 1915.
Disembarked, Basrah, 31st December, 1915.
Apptd. Transport Officer, 10th January, 1916.
Commanding Battn., 22nd to 23rd January, 1916.
Acting Adjutant, 24th January, 1916.
Invalided to India, 29th March, 1916.
Re-embarked, Karachi, 13th July, 1916.
Disembarked, Basrah, 16th July, 1916.
Invalided to India, 26th August, 1916.
Invalided to U. K., 4th October, 1916.

M. M. Thorburn, M. C.
Embarked, Marseilles, 5th December, 1915.
Disembarked, Basrah, 31st December, 1915.
Wounded in Action, 21st January, 1916.
Invalided to India, 4th February, 1916.
Awarded the Military Cross, January 1916.
Invalided to England from Egypt, 25th April, 1916.

Withey, R. W.
Posted to the Battalion, 6th December, 1917.

2ND LIEUTENANTS.

D. H. Anderson.
Embarked, Devonport, 16th February, 1916.
Disembarked, Basrah, 23rd March, 1916.
Killed in Action, 22nd April, 1916.

G. J. Anderson.
Embarked, Devonport, 16th February, 1910.
Disembarked, Basrah, 23rd March, 1916.
Killed in Action, 22nd April, 1916.

C. St. G. Alexander.
Embarked, Devonport, 16th February, 1916.
Disembarked, Basrah, 23rd March, 1916.
Invalided to India, 4th May, 1916.
(Wounded in Action, 22nd April, 1916).
To England from Egypt.

D. S. Gordon Brown.
Embarked, Bombay, 11th April, 1916.

Disembarked, Basrah, 17th April, 1916.
Accidentally wounded, 28th June, 1916.
Invalided to India, 5th August, 1916.

H. W. Bruce.
Embarked, Devonport, 16th February, 1916.
Disembarked, Basrah, 23rd March, 1916.
Invalided to India, 30th May, 1916.
Embarked, Karachi, 27th August, 1916.
Disembarked, Basrah, 2nd September, 1916.
Wounded in Action, 6th November, 1916.
Killed in Action, 17th February, 1917.

E. Bruce.
Embarked, Devonport, 16th February, 1916.
Disembarked, Basrah, 23rd March, 1916.
Invalided to India, 11th May, 1916.
Embarked, Karachi, 14th August, 1916.
Disembarked, Basrah, 20th August, 1916.
Died from Disease (Paratyphoid-A), 17th November, 1916.

A. E. Bairstow.
Embarked, Devonport, 9th October, 1916.
Disembarked, Basrah, 2nd December, 1916.

J. C. W. Broad.
Embarked, Marseilles, 5th December, 1915.
Disembarked, Basrah, 31st December, 1915.
Wounded in Action, 7th January, 1916.
Invalided to India, 16th January, 1916.
Re-embarked, Bombay, 22nd May, 1916.
Disembarked, Basrah, 30th May, 1916.
Invalided to India, 15th June, 1916.

K. Buchanan.
Embarked, Marseilles, 5th December, 1915.
Disembarked, Basrah, 31st December, 1915.
Wounded in Action, 7th January, 1916.
Invalided to India, 20th January, 1916.
Re-embarked, Bombay, 8th May, 1916.
Disembarked, Basrah, 16th May, 1916.
Invalided to India, 26th August, 1916.
Re-embarked, Bombay, 25th February, 1917.
Disembarked, Basrah, 4th March, 1917.

P. A. to Dir. of Port Admin. and Conservancy, 6th May, 1917.

J. C. R. Buchanan.
Embarked, Devonport, 9th February, 1917.
Disembarked, Basrah, 22nd May, 1917.

C. J. R. Brown.
Embarked, Karachi, 19th March, 1917.
Disembarked, Basrah, 26th March, 1917.
Wounded in Action, 21st April, 1917.
Died from Wounds, 21st May, 1917.

J. A. Byron.
Embarked, Karachi, 19th March, 1917.
Disembarked, Basrah, 26th March, 1917.

T. M. Cowie.
Embarked, Devonport, 15th October, 1916.
Disembarked, Basrah, 21st November, 1916.
Unofficially reported Pris. of War, 17th February, 1917.
Recaptured, 1st March, 1917.
(Wounded 17th February 1917).
Invalided to India, 15th March, 1917.

A. Crombie.
Embarked, Devonport, 26th April, 1916.
Disembarked, Basrah, 31st May, 1916.

J. H. Cotterell.
Embarked, Devonport, 10th February, 1916.
Disembarked, Basrah, 14th March, 1916.
Wounded in Action, 22nd April, 1916.
Invalided to India, 27th April, 1916.
Re-embarked, Bombay, 27th November, 1916.
Died from wounds, 15th March, 1917.

A. T. Downie.
Embarked, Bombay, 17th April, 1917.
Disembarked, Basrah, 23rd May, 1917.

J. Dawson.
Embarked, Devonport, 7th June, 1916.
Disembarked, Basrah, 4th July, 1916.
Invalided to India, 6th November, 1916.
Returned to England and died.

A. Douglas.
Embarked, Marseilles, 5th December, 1915.
Disembarked, Basrah, 31st December, 1915.
Wounded in Action, 13th January, 1916.
Reported dangerously ill, 18th January, 1916.
Died from Wounds, 9th February, 1916.

H. F. Forrester.
Embarked, Devonport, 10th February, 1916.
Disembarked, Basrah, 14th March, 1916.
Wounded and Missing, 22nd April, 1916.

T. Gant.
Promoted from C. S. M., 6th February, 1917.
Wounded in Action, 14th March, 1917.
To be A. Qr. Master., 12th May, 1917.

T. Gillespie.
Embarked, Devonport, 21st October, 1916.
Disembarked, Basrah, 21st November, 1916.
Killed in Action, 14th March, 1917.

J. F. Gillies.
Embarked, Devonport, 24th May, 1916.
Disembarked, Basrah, 13th June, 1916.
Invalided to India, 28th June, 1916.
To England, from Egypt, 30th September, 1916.

A. Gilroy.
Embarked, Devonport, 10th September, 1916.
Disembarked, Basrah, 10th October, 1916.
Wounded in Action, 21st April, 1917.
To be Lieutenant, 1st January, 1917.
Invalided to India, 18th May, 1917.

J. T. Grassie, D.S.O.
Embarked, Devonport, 20th January, 1916.
Disembarked, Basrah, 21st February, 1916.
Wounded in Action, 6th April, 1916.
Invalided to India, 10th April, 1916.
Invalided to U. K. from Egypt, 7th May, 1916.
Awarded the D.S.O., 22nd December, 1916.

K. Graham Scott.
Embarked, Devonport, 25th December, 1916.

Disembarked, Basrah, 9th March, 1917.

W. G. Grierson.
Embarked, Devonport, 5th January, 1917.
Disembarked, Basrah, 22nd March, 1917.

C. E. Gerrard.
Embarked, Karachi, 19th March, 1917.
Disembarked, Basrah, 26th March, 1917.

T. A. Henderson, M.C.
Embarked, Marseilles, 25th November, 1915.
Disembarked, Basrah, 28th December, 1915.
Wounded in Action, 7th January, 1916.
Awarded the Military Cross, 22nd December, 1916.
Awarded the Order of St.Vladimir, 4th Col., with Swords,
(*London Gaz.*, 5th July, 1917).
Invalided to India, 23rd May, 1917.

S. L. Hunter.
Embarked, Bombay, 27th July, 1916.
Disembarked, Basrah, 1st August, 1916.
Joined 3rd Echelon, as Record Officer, 22nd March, 1917.

B. S. Houston, M.C.
Promoted from C.S.M., 16th February, 1917.
Awarded the Military Cross, 31st March, 1917.

C. V. Hendry.
Embarked, Devonport, 7th June, 1916.
Disembarked, Basrah, 4th July, 1916.
Invalided to India, 6th November, 1916.

P. J. Haye.
Embarked, Devonport, 5th January, 1917.
Disembarked, Basrah, 22nd March, 1917.
D. Haig. Embarked, Devonport, 15th January, 1917,
Disembarked, Basrah, 21st March, 1917.
Invalided to India, 16th June, 1917.

M. Jamieson.
Embarked, Devonport, 9th October, 1916.
Disembarked, Basrah, 2nd December, 1916.

A. L. Jackson.
Posted to the Battalion, 28th August, 1917.

J. Jeff.
Embarked, Devonport, 24th May, 1917.
Disembarked, Basrah, 13th June, 1916.

A. S. Johnston.
Embarked, Bombay, 24th March, 1917.
Disembarked, Basrah, 28th March, 1917.

T. Kinnear.
Promoted from C.S.M., 6th February, 1917.
Wounded in Action, 22nd February, 1917.
Apptd. Transport Officer, 3rd May, 1917.

B. H. Lunn.
Embarked, Devonport, 24th May, 1916.
Disembarked, Basrah, 13th June, 1916.
Invalided to India, 8th December, 1916.
Has since been invalided to England.

T. Loudon.
Embarked, Devonport, 5th January, 1917.
Disembarked, Basrah, 22nd March, 1917.

J. Macgregor.
Posted to the Battalion, 13th September, 1917.

G. M. Mackenzie.
Embarked, Devonport, 24th May, 1916.
Disembarked, Basrah, 13th June, 1916.
Transferred to M. Gun Corps, 26th October, 1916.

Mann, J. A.
Posted to the Battalion, 6th December, 1917.

D. Murray Stewart.
Embarked, Devonport, 9th October, 1916.
Disembarked, Basrah, 2nd December, 1916.

R. S. Morrison.
Embarked, Marseilles, 5th December, 1915.
Disembarked, Basrah, 31st December, 1915.
Killed in Action, 7th January, 1916.

W. D. Montgomerie.
Embarked, Bombay, 17th May, 1917.
Disembarked, Basrah, 23rd May, 1917.

A. Muir.
Promoted from C.S.M., 29th May, 1917.

D. Mcarthur.
Embarked, Devonport, 5th January, 1917.
Disembarked, Basrah, 22nd March, 1917.
Died from Wounds, 21st April, 1917.

T. Peel.
Embarked, Devonport, 5th January, 1917.
Disembarked, Basrah, 22nd March, 1917.
Died from Wounds, 21st April, 1917.

J. C. Paterson.
Embarked, Marseilles, 5th December, 1915.
Disembarked, Basrah, 31st December, 1915.
Wounded in Action, 7th January, 1916.
Invalided to India, 16th January, 1916.
To England, from Egypt, 19th March, 1916.

W. Porter.
Posted to the Battalion, 21st November, 1917.

B. H. Quine.
Embarked, Devonport, 7th June, 1916.
Disembarked, Basrah, 4th July, 1916.
To be F. T. C. O., Dvn., 1st August, 1916.
Relieved from above, 26th August, 1916.
Invalided to India, 3rd September, 1916.

A. H. Quine.
Embarked, Karachi, 19th March, 1917.
Disembarked, Basrah, 26th March, 1917.
Reported Missing, 21st April, 1917.
Reported Pris. of War, 21st April, 1917.

G. Ryrie.
Embarked, Devonport, 11th July, 1916.
Disembarked, Basrah, 10th August, 1916.
Invalided to India, 28th November, 1916.
Re-embarked, Bombay, 27th May, 1917.
Disembarked, Basrah, 4th June, 1917.

J. C. Ritchie, M. C.
Embarked, Devonport, 5th January, 1917.
Disembarked, Basrah, 22nd March, 1917.
Awarded the Military Cross, 22nd May, 1917.
Apptd. A. Adjt., 27th May, 1917.

A. Scobie.
Posted to the Battalion, 13th September, 1917.

A. E. Sinclair.
Embarked Devonport, 24th May, 1916.
Disembarked, Basrah, 13th June, 1916.
Transferred to M. Gun Corps, 26th October, 1916.
Killed in Action, 5th December, 1916.

P. J. Scotland.
Posted To the Battalion, 9th December, 1917.

G. V. Stewart.
Embarked, Bombay, 11th April, 1916.
Disembarked, Basrah, 17th April, 1916.
Wounded in Action, 14th March, 1917.

G. B. Smart.
Embarked, Suez, 16th September, 1916.
Disembarked, Basrah, 26th September, 1916.
Wounded in Action, 14th March, 1917.

F. H. Soutar
Embarked, Marseilles, 25th November, 1915.
Disembarked, Basrah, 28th December, 1915.
Killed in Action, 21st January, 1916.

T. L. Smith.
Posted to the Battalion, 13th September, 1917.

P. E. Symthe.
Embarked, Devonport, 9th October, 1916.
Disembarked, Basrah, 2nd December, 1916.
Confirmed in rank of 2nd Lieutenant, 18th October 1916.
Wounded in Action, 21st April, 1917.
Invalided to India, 12th June, 1917.

R. M. Smythe.
Embarked, Devonport, 9th October, 1916.
Disembarked, Basrah, 14th December, 1916.
Wounded in Action, 14th March, 1917.
Confirmed in rank of 2nd Lieut., 18th October, 1916.

A. G. Woyka.
Embarked, Devonport, 26th April, 1916.
Disembarked, Basrah, 31st May, 1916.
Invalided to India, 15th January, 1917.

R. Walker.

Embarked, Karachi, 19th March, 1917.

Disembarked, Basrah, 26th March, 1917.

Killed in Action, 21st April, 1917.

A. A. Young.

Embarked, Devonport, 24th May 1916.

Disembarked, Basrah, 13th June, 1916.

Cypher Officer, G. H. Q. Base, 28th June, 1916.

Joined Bn. in the Fd., 25th November, 1916.

Died from Wounds, 14th March, 1917.

Nominal roll of W.Os., N.C.Os., and men, 2nd Bn., numerically arranged, who have been killed in action, died of wounds, disease, etc., during service in Mesopotamia, from 1st January 1916 to 15th June 1917.

Regtl. No.	Rank and Name.	Cause of Death.	Date of Death.	Place of Death.	Place of burial, if known.
72	Sergt. T. Archer	K. in A.	22-4-16	The Field.	Probably Sann-i-yat battlefield (G.R.C.).
AR/116	A/Cpl. D. Dakers	"	22-4-16	"	" " "
133	Sergt. T. Murray	"	7-1-16	"	Probably Sheikh-Saad (G.R.C.).
578	A/Cpl. J. Gibb	"	21-1-16	"	Probably Hannah battlefield (G.R.C.).
598	Pte. J. Hogg	"	21-1-16	"	" " "
622	Pte. J. Lynch	"	7-1-16	"	Probably Sheikh-Saad (G.R.C.).
672	Corpl. R. Pratt	"	7-1-16	"	" " "
773	L/Cpl. R. Whyte	"	6-11-16	"	Cemetery near Jullundur St. Sann-i-yat.
781	Corpl. U. Hutchison	"	21-4-17	"	Dujail battlefield, T.C. 97, Sq. G-7,
797	Pte. A. Milne	"	21-4-17	"	7th Divn., Sketch No. 5, Istabulat.
814	Pte. G. McAulay	"	21-1-16	"	Orah battlefield, Map L-2, Rev. Irwin.
896	Sergt. G. Johnston	"	22-4-16	"	...
981	Pte. G. Hazeldean	"	21-1-16	"	Orah battlefield, Map L-2, Rev. Irwin.
1020	L/Sgt. J. Mulholland	"	7-1-16	"	Probably Sheikh-Saad (G.R.C.).
1038	Pte. T. McFarlane	"	7-1-16	"	" " "
1060	L/Sgt. J. Inglis	"	7-1-16	"	" " "
1207	L/Cpl. A. Brown	"	7-1-16	"	" " "
1335	L/Cpl. A. Cowie	"	21-4-17	"	Point 40-22, T.C. 97 Sq. G-7, Istabulat.
					Probably Sheikh-Saad

No.	Name	Rank	Date	Place	Notes
1418	L/Cpl. W. Mack	"	22-4-16	"	Probably Sann-i-yat battlefield (G.R.C.).
1426	Pte. A. Reoch	"	7-1-16	"	Probably Sheikh-Saad (G.R.C).
1449	Piper J. Davis	"	25-9-15	France.	...
1452	Pte. J. Smith	"	14-3-17	The Field.	...
1472	Sergt. R. Madill	"	7-1-16	"	Probably Sheikh-Saad (G.R.C.).
1591	Sergt. D. Hamilton	"	7-1-16	"	" " "
1619	L/Cpl. W. Noble	"	14-3-17	"	...
1642	A/Sgt. D. Neill	"	22-4-16	"	Probably Sann-i-yat battlefield (G.R.C).
1701	Sergt. T. Henderson	"	7-1-16	"	Probably Sheikh-Saad (G.R.C).
1714	L/Cpl. D. Duke	"	22-4-16	"	...
1780	Sergt. D. Finlay, V.C.	"	21-1-16	"	Probably Hannah battlefield (G.R.C).
1791	Pte. G. Burness	"	7-1-16	"	Probably Sheikh-Saad (G.R.C).
1856	A/Cpl. D. Hughes	"	21-1-16	"	Probably Hannah battlefield (G.R.C.).
1859	A/C. S.M.T. Bissett	"	14-3-17	"	...
1884	Corpl. R. Speed	"	21-4-17	"	Point 40-22 T.C. 97 Sq. G-7 Istabulat.
1899	Pte. Craig, R.	"	14-3-17	"	...
2003	Pte. T. Teirney	"	23-6-16	"	...
2029	A/Sgt. A. Kiddle	"	21-1-16	"	Probably Hannah battlefield (G.R.C.).
2084	Sergt. J. Barrie	"	14-3-17	"	...
3/2160	Corpl. W. Gow	"	20-4-16	"	Probably Sann-i-yat battlefield (G.R.C.).
2185	Dmr. G. Bullion	"	6-4-16	"	" " "
2277	L/Cpl. W. Grimmond	"	22-4-16	"	" " "
2316	A/Sergt. T. Marshall	"	21-1-16	"	Probably Hannah battlefield (G.R.C.).
2451	L/Cpl. N. Campbell	"	7-1-16	"	Probably Sheikh-Saad (G.R.C.).
3/2496	Pte. H. Duffy	"	22-4-16	"	Probably Sann-i-yat battlefield (G.R.C.).
3/2508	Pte. S. Mowat	"	22-1-16	"	Orah battlefield, Map L-2, Rev. Irwin.
2511	A/Cpl. D. Simpson	"	14-3-17	"	...
3/2519	Pte. J Downie	"	7-1-16	"	Probably Sheikh-Saad battlefield (G.R.C.).
3/2520	L/Cpl. C. Low	"	7-1-16	"	" " "
2545	Corpl. T. Brown	"	22-4-16	"	Probably Sann-i-yat battlefield (G.R.C.).
3/2564	L/Cpl. G. Mitchell	"	13-1-16	"	Orah battlefield, Map L-2, Rev. Irwin.
3/2569	Pte. B. Cunningham	"	22-4-16	"	Probably Sann-i-yat battlefield (G.R.C.).

3/2585	Pte. R. McQuarrie	"	22-4-16	"	" " "
3/2584	Pte. J. O'Donnell	"	21-4-17	"	Point 40-22 T.C. 97, Sq. G-7. Istabulat (G.R.C.).
3/2614	Pte. J. Black	"	22-4-16	"	Probably Sann-i-yat battlefield (G.R.C)
3/2621	Pte. J. Cook	"	6-4-16	"	" " "
3/2632	Pte. E. Clark	"	13-1-16	"	Orah battlefield, Map L-2, Rev. Irwin.
3/2674	Pte. G. Stevenson	"	7-1-16	"	Probably Sheikh-Saad battlefield, (G.R.C).
2701	Pte. F. Gibo	"	22-4-16	"	Probably Sann-i-yat battlefield (G.R.C).
2745	Pte. L. Phee	"	7-1-16	"	Probably Sheikh-Saad battlefield, (G.R.C).
3/3012	Pte. A. Hay	"	14-3-17	"	...
3/3074	Pte. P. Glancy	"	21-1-16	"	Probably Hannah battlefield (G.R.C).
3/3100	Pte. T. Burke	"	21-4-17	"	...
S/3342	Sergt. J. Lees	"	14-3-17	"	...
3/3360	Pte. J. Campbell	"	9-5-15	France.	
3380	Pte. J. Strachan	"	22-4-16	The Field.	Probably Sann-i-yat battlefield (G.R.C.).
3/3471	Pte. J. Harman	"	22-4-16	"	" " "
3/3590	Pte. G. Forbes	"	22-4-16	"	" " "
3874	Pte. R. Wilson	"	6-4-16	"	" " "
3/3917	Pte. F. Robertson	"	22-4-16	"	" " "
S/4144	Pte. A. Mailer	"	7-1-16	"	Probably Sheikh-Saad battlefield (G.R.C).
S/4151	Pte. E. Harkness	"	22-4-16	"	Probably Sann-i-yat battlefield (G.R.C).
S/4221	Pte. E. Graham	"	21-4-17	"	Point 40-22 T.C. 97, Sq. G-7, Istabulat.
3/4222	Pte. D. Cuthbert	"	21-1-16	"	Probably Hannah battlefield (G.R.C.).
S/4484	L/Cpl. J. Shirra	"	21-4-17	"	Dujail battlefield, T.C. 97, Sq. G-7, Istabulat (G.R.C).
S/5142	Pte. J. Bennett	"	14-3-17	"	...
S/6113	Pte. J. Stuart	"	22-4-16	"	Probably Sann-i-yat battlefield (G.R.C).
S/6259	Pte. F. Stafford	"	22-4-16	"	Probably Sann-i-yat battlefield (G.R.C.).
S/6405	L/Cpl. T. Weir	"	13-3-16	"	Probably Hannah battlefield (G.R.C.).
S/6415	Pte. A. Rogerson	"	22-4-16	"	Probably Sann-i-yat battlefield (G.R.C.).
S/6652	Pte. P. Hughes	"	22-4-16	"	...
S/6711	Pte. G. Jones	"	7-1-16	"	Probably Sheikh-Saad battlefield (G.R.C.).
S/6757	L/Cpl. W. Taylor	"	21-1-16	"	Probably Hannah battlefield (G.R.C.).
6818	Pte. T. Caddow	"	14-3-17	"	...
S/6958	Pte. E. McLure	"	21-1-16	"	Probably Hannah battlefield (G.R.C.).
S/7009	L/Cpl. J. Gibson	"	9-8-16	"	...

S/7019	Pte. J. Hay	"	21-4-17	"	Point 40-22, T.C. 97, Sq. G-7, Istabul.
S/7088	A/Sgt. R. McLauchan	"	13-1-16	"	Orah battlefield, Map. L-2, Rev. Irwin.
S/7094	Pte. J. Coulter	"	7-1-16	"	Probably Sheikh-Saad battlefield, (G.R.C.).
S/7097	L/Cpl. C. McRae	"	7-1-16	"	Probably Sheikh-Saad battlefield, (G.R.C.).
7100	L/Cpl. F. Wilkins	"	7-1-16	"	Probably Sheikh-Saad battlefield, (G.R.C.).
S/7283	Pte. D. Bell	"	22-4-16	"	Probably Sann-i-yat battlefield, (G.R.C).
S/7346	Pte. A. Dickson	"	22-4-16	"	...
S/7507	Pte. W. McKennie	"	7-1-16	"	...
S/7508	Pte. T. Lamb	"	7-1-16	"	Probably Sheikh-Saad battlefield (G.R.C.).
S/7548	Pte. A. McKay	"	14-3-17	"	...
S/7560	Pte. J. Tarberts	"	22-4-16	"	Probably Sann-i-yat battlefield (G.R.C).
S/7580	Pte. J. Baillie	"	22-4-16	"	...
S/7592	Pte. R. Bowman	"	7-1-16	"	Probably Sheikh-Saad battlefield (G.R.C.).
S/7595	Pte. G. Drysdale	"	6-4-16	"	Probably Sann-i-yat battlefield (G.R.C).
S/7616	L/Cpl. J. McLaughlan	"	21-1-16	"	Probably Hannah battlefield (G.R.C.).
S/7738	Pte. A. Moncur	"	7-1-16	"	Probably Sheikh-Saad battlefield (G.R.C.).
S/7743	Pte. A. Mann	"	14-3-17	"	...
S/7748	Pte. T. McPherson	"	7-1-16	"	Probably Sheikh-Saad battlefield (G.R.C.).
S/7757	Pte. W. Gillispie	"	22-4-16	"	Probably Sann-i-yat battlefield (G.R.C.).
S/7771	C.-S.-M. D. Palmer	"	21-4-17	"	Dujail battlefield, T.C. 97, Sq. G-7, Istabulat.
7912	C.-S.-M. R. Proudfoot	"	21-1-16	"	Probably Hannah battlefield (G.R.C.).
S/7926	Pte. J. McCormack	"	22-4-16	"	Probably Sann-i-yat battlefield (G.R.C.).
S/7943	Pte. W. Beatte	"	21-1-16	"	Probably Hannah battlefield (G.R.C.).
S/7957	Pte. J. Whyte	"	21-1-16	"	" " "
S/7967	Pte. E. Brown	"	22-4-16	"	...
S/7994	Corpl. A. Critchton	"	22-4-16	"	Probably Sann-i-yat battlefield (G.R.C.).
S/7996	Pte. W. Graham	"	7-1-16	"	Probably Sheikh-Saad battlefield (G.R.C.).
S/8057	Pte. J. Thomson	"	21-1-16	"	Probably Hannah battlefield (G.R.C.).
S/8062	Pte. D. Hardley	"	22-4-16	"	...
S/8082	Pte. J. Ramsay	"	22-4-16	"	Probably Sann-i-yat battlefield (G.R.C.).
8169	Pte. E. Rooke	"	7-1-16	"	Probably Sheikh-Saad battlefield (G.R.C.).

S/8192	Pte. M. McMahon	"	22-4-16	"	...
S/8202	Pte. D. Winter	"	21-4-17	"	Point 40-22 T.C. 97, Sq. G-7, Istabulat.
8235	Pte. R. Lindsay	"	22-4-16	"	Probably Sann-i-yat battlefield (G.R.C.).
S/8252	Pte. D. Kilgour	"	21-1-16	"	Probably Hannah battlefield (G.R.C.).
S/8316	Pte. S. McKillop	"	7-1-16	"	
S/8329	Pte. J. Suttie	"	6-3-16	"	Probably Hannah battlefield (G.R.C.).
S/8330	Pte. G. Smith	"	7-1-16	"	Probably Sheikh-Saad battlefield (G.R.C.).
S/8349	L/Cpl. A. Cochrane	"	14-3-17	"	...
S/8389	Pte. J. Clark	"	22-4-16	"	Probably Sann-i-yat battlefield (G.R.C.).
S/8390	Corpl. P. Robertson	"	7-1-16	"	Probably Sheikh-Saad battlefield (G.R.C.).
S/8428	Pte. J. Wilson	"	7-1-16	"	Probably Sheikh-Saad battlefield (G.R.C.).
S/8444	Sergt. A. McDonald	"	21-1-16	"	Probably Hannah battlefield (G.R.C.).
8458	A/Cpl. J. Hughes	"	21-1-16	"	Probably Hannah battlefield (G.R.C.).
S/8500	Pte. W. McNee	"	22-4-16	"	Probably Sann-i-yat battlefield (G.R.C.).
S/8534	Pte. R. McDonald	"	22-4-16	"	Probably Sann-i-yat battlefield (G.R.C.).
S/8551	Pte. A. Gibson	"	21-4-17	"	Point 40-22, T.C. 97, Sq. G-7, Istabulat (G.K.C.).
S/8571	L/Cpl. D. McPhee	"	7-1-16	"	...
S/8696	Pte. J. Bell	"	7-1-16	"	Probably Sheikh-Saad battlefield (G.R.C.).
S/8705	Pte. F. Fraser	"	7-1-16	"	Probably Sheikh-Saad battlefield (G.R.C.).
S/8765	Pte. J. Stewart	"	18-6-16	"	...
S/8785	Pte. J. Liddle	"	21-4-17	"	Point 40-22, T.C. 97, Sq. G-7, Istabulat.
S/8867	Pte. J. Smith	"	7-1-16	"	Probably Sheikh-Saad battlefield (G.R.C.).
S/8890	Pte. T. Cranston	"	13-1-16	"	Orah battlefield, Map L-2, Rev. Irwin.
S/8918	Pte. J. Lamb	"	22-4-16	"	Probably Sann-i-yat battlefield (G.R.C).
S/9194	A/Cpl. J. Dougal	"	21-1-16	"	Probably Hannah battlefield (G.R.C.).
S/9207	Pte. J. Orr	"	7-1-16	"	Probably Sheikh-Saad battlefield (G.R.C.).
S/9231	Pte. T. Reid	"	22-4-16	"	Probably Sann-i-yat battlefield (G.R.C).
S/9339	Pte. T. Williamson	"	20-4-17	"	...

Number	Name		Date		Location
9383	Sergt. D. Murdoch	"	21-4-17	"	Dujail battlefield, point 40-22 T.C. 97. Sq. G-7, Istabulat.
9437	C.-S.-M. G. Davidson	"	7-1-16	"	Probably Sheikh-Saad (G.R.C).
9451	Pte. P. Davie	"	7-1-16	"	Probably Sheikh-Saad (G.R.C).
S/9504	Pte. C. Low	"	22-4-16	"	Probably Sann-i-yat battlefield (G.R.C).
S/9544	Segt. T. McCutcheon	"	22-4-16	"	Probably Sann-i-yat battlefield (G.R.C).
S/9563	Pte. C. Thomson	"	22-4-16	"	Probably Sann-i-yat battlefield (G.R.C).
S/9643	Pte. H. Fraser	"	22-4-16	"	Probably Sann-i-yat battlefield (G.R.C).
S/9952	Pte. C. Turner	"	14-3-17	"	...
S/10006	Pte. J. Ross	"	7-1-16	"	Probably Sheikh-Saad (G.R.C).
S/10028	Pte. J. Barnes	"	21-4-17	"	Point 40-22, T.C. 97, Sq. G-7, Istabulat. Orah battlefield, Map L-2,
SRA/10	Pte. T. Belcher	"	13-2-16	"	Rev. Irwin.
S/10170	Pte. E. Holmes	"	21-1-18	"	Probably Hannah battlefield (G.R.C).
10240	L/C. A. Gibson	"	21-4-17	"	Point 40-22, T.C. 97, Sq. G-7, Istabulat.
SRA/10	Pte. B. Wilson	"	7-1-16	"	Probably Sheikh-Saad (G.R.C.).
SRA/10	Pte. E. Kenny	"	14-3-17	"	...
S/10340	Pte. J. Dick	"	7-1-16	"	Probably Sheikh-Saad (G.R.C.).
S/10374	Pte. P. Paul	"	7-1-16	"	" " "
SRA/10	L-Cpl. A. Robertson	"	7-1-16	"	" " "
S/10469	Pte. R. Barrie	"	22-4-16	"	Probably Sann-i-yat battlefield (G.R.C).
S/10477	Pte. A. Graham	"	21-4-17	"	Point 40-22, T.C. 97, Sq. G-7, Istabulat.
S/10480	Pte. W. Ballingall	"	13-1-16	"	Orah battlefield, Map L-2, Rev. Irwin.
S/10482	Pte. D. McFarlane	"	7-1-16	"	Probably Sheikh-Saad (G.R.C).
10489	Pte. J. Sims	"	7-1-16	"	" " "
S/10537	L/Cpl. W. Malcolm	"	22-4-16	"	Probably Sann-i-yat battlefield (G.R.C).
S/10539	L/Cpl. P. Hardie	"	22-4-16	"	" " "
S/10545	Pte. T. Baillie	"	5-12-16	"	Jullundur St. Cemetery, Sann-i-yat (G.R.C.).
S/10564	Pte. J. Dalton	"	21-1-17	"	Dujail battlefield, T.C. 97, Sq. G-7, Istabulat.
S/10566	Pte. D. McLean	"	14-3-17	"	...
S/10567	Pte. J. Dawson	"	22-4-16	"	Probably Sann-i-yat battlefield (G.R.C).
S/10574	Pte. K. O'Donnell	"	22-4-16	"	" " "
S/10586	Pte. M. Paul	"	22-4-16	"	" " "
S/10592	Pte. E. Smith	"	22-4-16	"	" " "

S/10598 L/Cpl. J. McKay	"	22-4-16	"	"	"	"		
S/10621 Pte. W. Lang	"	22-4-16	"	"	"	"		
S/10633 Pte. W. Watson	"	5-11-16	"	Jullundur St. Cemetery, Sann-i-yat (G.R.C.).				
S/10634 L/Cpl. P. Reilly	"	17-3-17	"	...				
S/10638 Pte. F. Inglis	"	22-4-16	"	Probably Sann-i-yat battlefield (G.R.C).				
S/10648 Pte. J. Wylie	"	22-4-16	"	"	"	"		
S/10651 L/Cpl. D. Small	"	22-4-16	"	"	"	"		
S/10656 Pte. P. Barnes	"	22-4-16	"	"	"	"		
S/11147 A/Cpl. J. Harkins	"	22-4-16	"	"	"	"		
S/11175 L/Cpl. J. Little	"	22-4-16	"	"	"	"		
S/11193 Pte. J. Clark	"	14-3-17	"	...				
S/11305 Pte. J. McLean	"	13-4-16	"	Probably Sann-i-yat battlefield (G.R.C).				
S/11333 Pte. J. Galbraith	"	14-10-16	"	Cemetery at 28 B.F.A., Faliheyah Bend.				
S/11369 Pte. R. Niven	"	24-4-16	"	...				
S/11532 Pte. A. Huitton	"	21-4-17	"	Point 40-22, T.C. 97, Sq. G-7, Istabulat.				
				Probably Sann-i-yat				
S/11533 Pte. B. Bogan	"	22-4-16	"	battlefield (G.R.C).				
S/11570 Pte. J. Smith	"	22-4-16	"	"	"	"		
S/11572 Pte. J. Stewart	"	22-4-16	"	"	"	"		
S/11613 Pte. H. Greenwood	"	14-3-17	"	...				
S/11631 L/Cpl. J. Wallace	"	14-3-17	"	...				
S/11669 Pte. G. Law	"	21-4-17	"	Point 40-22, T.C. 97, Sq. G-7, Istabulat.				
S/11673 Pte. G. Hayes	"	16-6-16	"	...				
S/11726 Pte. A. Carmichael	"	22-4-16	"	Probably Sann-i-yat battlefield (G.R.C).				
S/11371 Pte. C. Wilson	"	22-4-16	"	"	"	"		
S/11866 Pte. T. Galloway	"	21-4-17	"	Point 40-22, T.C. 97, Sq. G-7, Istabulat.				
S/11869 Pte. J. Studholme	"	22-4-16	"	Probably Sann-i-yat battlefield (G.R.C).				
S/11891 Pte. D. Mathers	"	14-3-17	"	...				
S/11958 Pte. R. McNaughten	"	21-4-17	"	Dujail battlefield, T.C. 97, Sq. G-7, 7th Division, sketch No. 5, Istabulat.				
S/12096 Pte. W. Cross	"	21-4-17	"	Dujail battlefield, T.C. 97, Sq. G-7, 7th Division, sketch No. 5, Istabulat.				
S/12202 L/Cpl. E. Doggett	"	14-3-17	"	...				
S/12238 Pte. D. McCraw	"	11-12-16	"	Jullundur St. Cemetery. Sann-i-yat.				
S/12395 Pte. A. Johnstone	"	21-4-17	"	...				
S/12435 Pte. W. Jamieson	"	21-4-17	"	Point 40-22, Sq. G-7, T.C. 97, Istabulat.				
S/12475 Pte. J. Keir	"	22-4-16	"	Probably Sann-i-yat battlefield (G.R.C).				
S/12494 Pte. A. Tuckerman	"	14-3-17	"	...				
S/13111 Pte. A. Smith	"	14-3-17	"	...				

No.	Name		Date	Unit		Burial Place
S/15068	Pte. J. Lawson	"	21-4-17		"	Point 40-22, T.C. 97, Sq. G-7, Istabulat.
S/15069	Pte. J. McLeod	"	14-3-17		"	...
S/15127	Pte. W. Coyne	"	21-4-17		"	Dujail battlefield, T.C. 97, G-7, 7th Division, sketch No. 5, Istabulat.
S/15537	Pte. J. Gemmell	"	21-4-17		"	" " "
S/15632	Pte. J. Adam	"	21-4-17		"	" " "
S/15700	Pte. G. Crick	"	14-3-17		"	...
S/15853	Pte. J. Wiseman	"	14-3-17		"	...
S/15866	Pte. W. McKay	"	14-3-17		"	...
S/16233	Pte. P. Dair	"	14-3-17		"	...
16303	L/Cpl. P. McSkimming	"	11-2-17		"	Jullundur St. Cemetery, Sann-i-yat.
S/16353	Pte. H. McKay	"	14-3-17		"	...
17481	Corpl. H. Bowman	"	14-3-17		"	...
17483	Pte. J. Eglin	"	14-3-17		"	...
S/19311	Pte. G. Neilson	"	21-4-17		"	Point 40-22, T.C. 97, Sq. G-7, Istabulat.
S/19316	Pte. J. Sanderson	"	21-4-17		"	...
19426	Pte. J. Clark	"	21-4-17		"	Point 40-22, T.C. 97, Sq. G-7, Istabulat.
19435	Pte. D. Aitken	"	14-3-17		"	...
19436	Pte. J. Crawford	"	17-2-17		"	Jullundur St. Cemetery, Sann-i-yat.
19450	Corpl. L. Wiseman	"	21-4-17		"	Point 40-22, T.C. 97, Sq. G-7, Istabulat.
19456	Pte. J. Wilkinson	"	21-4-17		"	" " "
69	L/Cpl. A. McBurnie	Died fr. Wds.	9-1-16		"	...
79	Pte. E. Miller	"	20-4-17	19 Cas. Cl. Stn.		Sindiyeh Cemetery, T.C. 87, Sq. 1-H.
3/471	Pte. W. Taggart	"	16-1-16	No. 5 Fd. Amb.		...
828	Sergt. A. Downie	"	5-5-16	3 B. G. H., Amara.		...
941	A/Cpl. R. McNee	"	22-1-16	3a B. G. H., Amara.		...
1305	Pte. J. Macrae	"	30-1-16	3a B. G. H., Amara.		...
1381	Pte. G. Hendric	"	30-1-16	3a B. G. H., Amara.		...
3/1755	Pte. P. McPhee	"	24-4-16	The Field.		...
1831	Pte. A. Mauby	"	17-1-16	No. 2 B.G.H., Amara.		...
1947	Pte. T. Morrison	"	6-4-16	The Field.		...
3/2112	Pte. J. Welsh	"	11-4-17	32 B. G. H., Amara.		Amara Cemetery, Row No. II,.A, Grave No. 13.
2117	L/Cpl. R. McBean	"	8-2-16	3a B.G.H., Basra.		Basra.
2145	Sergt. G. McGregor	"	7-12-16	20 B.F.A.		Br. Cemetery at 20 B.F.A., Falaheyeh, Row. No. 4.
3/2312	Pte. H. Dand	"	24-4-16	3a B.G.H., Basra.		...
2355	L/Cpl. J. Cunningham	"	16-3-17	The Field.		Hassiawah, (15 mls. N. of Baghdad).

No.	Name		Date	Unit/Field	Remarks
2381	Pte. W. Gibb	"	22-1-16	"	...
3/2647	Pte. A. Robertson	"	15-1-16	3a B.G.H., Amara.	...
2675	Pte. F. Morrison	"	15-3-17	The Field.	...
3/2742	Pte. H. McMillan	"	19-12-16	20 B.F.A.	Cemetery at 20 B.F.A.
S/2876	Pte. R. Brown	"	24-4-17	130 I.F.A.	...
S/2903	Pte. W. Marshall	"	22-4-16	The Field.	...
S/2920	Pte. J. Anderson	"	24-1-17	"	Chabela Mound Cemetery. T.C. 61, 16c, 48, 19, Grave No. 2.
S/3198	Pte. J. Forbes	"	12-4-16	R-P. B.G.H., Amara.	...
S/3358	L/Cpl. D. Richardson	"	25-4-16	S.S. Mejidieh.	...
3/3362	Pte. T. Welsh	"	3-5-16	3 B.G.H., Amara.	...
S/3755	Pte. A. Ettrick	"	24-4-16	S.S. Mejidieh.	...
S/3934	Pte. A. Fleming	"	25-4-16	3a B.G.H., Amara.	...
S/4004	Pte. B. Evans	"	27-4-16	3a B.G.H., Amara.	Amara.
S/4093	Corpl. J. Gillies	"	22-4-16	The Field.	...
S/4218	Pte. W. Mackie	"	24-4-16	"	...
S/5230	Pte. J. McDougall	"	17-2-17	"	Jullundur St. Cemetery, Sann-i-yat.
S/5658	Pte. T. S.	"	26-4-16	S.S. Mejedeih.	
S/6436	Pte. F. Bewley	"	24-3-17	3a B.S.H. S-Sd.	Sheikh-Saad Cemetery, Row 6, Gr. No. 364.
S/6689	Pte. W. Dewar	"	18-2-16	3a B.G.H. Basra.	...
S/6964	A/Cpl. G. Combe	"	6-3-17	23 B.S.H. Amara.	Amara Cemetery, Grave No. VII, 6, 7.
S/6972	H. Rodgers	"	6-9-16	The Field.	Cemetery at 20 B.F.A.
S/7122	Pte. A. Lamont	"	25-1-16	3a B.G.H. Amara.	...
S/7207	L/Cpl. J. Young	"	5-3-16	3 B.G.H. Amara.	...
S/7399	Pte. D. Urquhart	"	20-4-16	The Field.	...
S/7427	Pte. A. Rae	"	8-1-16	"	...
S/7430	A/Cpl. D. Moncreiff	"	13-1-16	"	...
S/7479	Pte. J. Shannon	"	19-1-16	3 B.G.H., Amara.	...
S/7538	Pte. M. Stewart	"	14-3-17	The Field.	...
S/7730	Pte. J. Stewart	"	22-6-16	"	...
8175	Sergt. J. Lugton	"	15-3-17	Motor Convoy. 128 I.F.A.	5 miles N. of Tagi Rly. Stn. and 40 E. of railway line.
S/8183	Pte. F. Scott	"	22-4-16	The Field.	...
S/8266	Pte. W. Stewart	"	8-1-16	"	Probably Sheikh-Saad (G.R.C).
S/8356	Pte. A. Trory	"	7-9-16	"	...
S/8709	Pte. J. Ferguson	"	14-1-16	2 B.G.H., Amara.	...
S/8856	Pte. J. Elliott	"	22-4-16	The Field.	...
S/9159	Pte. C. Wilson	"	24-4-16	"	...
S/9728	L/Cpl. E. Thomson	"	15-3-17	128 I.F.A.	...
RA/100	Pte. J. Davy	"	24-4-16	The Field.	...
S/10155	Pte. P. Welsh	"	8-1-16	"	...

SRA/10	Pte. A. Harker	"	8-1-16	"	...
S/10432	Pte. T. Wilson	"	15-3-17	128 I.F.A.	5 miles N. of Tagi Station and 40 E. of Railway.
RA/104	Pte. W. Hallam	"	14-4-17	32 B.G.H., Amara.	Amara Cemetery, Grave No. II, A, 14.
S/10639	Pte. J. Walker	"	27-4-16	3a B.G.H., Basra.	...
S/10652	L/Cpl. A. Kay	"	24-5-17	32 B.G.H., Amara.	...
S/10654	L/Cpl. C. Williams	"	24-4-16	The Field.	
S/11259	Pte. P. Hiley	"	29-4-16	3a B.G.H., Amara.	...
S/11535	Pte. D. Smith	"	22-4-16	The Field.	...
S/11769	Pte. J. Nicol	"	1-6-16	"	Cemetery at 20 B.F.A.
S/12162	Pte. W. Cannell	"	24-4-17	130 I.F.A.	...
S/12321	L/Cpl. L. Latto	"	23-4-17	No. 7 B.F.A.	T.C. 96, 6-E, 3-1.
S/12512	Pte. A. Swanston	"	24-2-17	The Field.	
S/13103	Pte. W. Benson	"	22-4-17	No. 19 B.F.A.	S.-E. of Ry. culvert about 4-3/4 miles S.-E. of Istabulat Station, T.C. 97, K-9, 5-6.
13186	L/Cpl. W. Campbell	"	15-3-17	128 I.F.A.	...
S/13260	Pte. W. Nelson	"	14-3-17	The Field.	...
S/13325	Pte. T. Simpson	"	14-3-17	"	...
S/14626	Pte. T. Hanvey	"	23-4-17	130 I.F.A.	...
S/16060	Pte. C. Ogilvie	"	25-4-17	16 C.C.S.	Grave No. A-22 (Cemetery unknown).
S/16041	Pte. C. Gray	"	26-4-17	32 B.G.H.	Amara Cemetery, Grave VIII, Block B-1.
S/16082	Pte. P. Glen	"	9-5-17	2 B.G.H.	...
S/16323	Pte. A. Thompson	"	20-5-17	32 B.G.H.	...
19445	Pte. D. Porter	"	21-4-17	19 B.F.A.	...
1062	Sgt. W. Hanton	Enteric.	6-7-16	3 B.G.H.	...
513	L/Cpl. G. Robertson	Suffocati	24-1-16	The Field.	...
1549	Pte. J. Bennett	Dysenter	21-9-16	Sheikh-Saad.	Sheikh-Saad Cemetery, Grave No. F-59.
3/2008	Pte. D. Mathieson	Gastritis.	18-6-17	Falaheyeh.	Cemetery at 26 B.F.A.
3/2475	A/Sgt. W. Chrystal	Sun-stroke.	19-6-16	Kurna.	Christian burial ground, Kurna, Row B, Grave 11.
2750	Dmr. J. Watt	Para-typh.	10-7-16	Sheikh-Saad.	Sheikh-Saad Cemetery, Grave No. 105.
3/3572	Pte. G. Billington	"	1-7-16	"	" " "
3892	Pte. J. Sanderson	Disease.	29-6-16	S.S. Malamir.	...
3/4229	Pte. J. Clark	Heat-stroke.	26-7-16	Amara.	...
3/4246	Pte. T. Clowe	P.U.O.	7-7-16	"	...
3/4251	Pte. P. McGinley	Suffocati	27-6-16	"	...
3/4252	Pte. S. Johnstone	Enteric.	4-7-16	"	...
S/4874	Pte. J. Fettes	Gastritis.	20-7-16	Falaheyeh.	Cemetery at 20 B.F.A.
S/6709	Pte. W. Sherriff	Enteritis.	27-5-16	"	...
3/7229	Pte. E. Dunbar	Heat-stroke.	3-7-16	3 B.G.H.	...

S/7622	Pte. W. Ferguson	Enteric.	3-10-16	33 B.G.H.	...
S/7643	Pte. E. Wallace	Heat-stroke.	20-7-16	Basrah.	...
S/8024	Pte. A. McLaren	Dysenter	29-5-16	3 B.G.H.	...
S/8040	Pte. S. Russell	"	21-6-16	R. Boat P-4.	...
8052	Sgt. G. Warden	Enteric.	26-5-17	127 C.F.A.	...
8390	Pte. W. Murphy	Typhus.	20-4-17	Amara.	Amara Cemetery, Grave No. VIII, A. 5.

Drowned

S/8713	L/Cpl. J. Cairney	Acc.	14-3-16	The Field.	...
S/8715	Pte. J. Oliphant	N.Y.D. fever.	17-8-16	Sheikh-Saad.	...
S/8888	Pte. D. Fleming	Malaria.	2-8-16	The Field.	...
9852	Pte. J. Beattie	Dysenter	30-12-16	33 B.G.H.	Hakimeyeh Cemetery, Makina, Row C, No. 15.
S/10012	Pte. R. Cowper	Cholera.	19-5-16	The Field.	...
S/10047	Pte. R. Broadbent	Heat-stroke.	1-7-16	Falaheyeh.	Cemetery at 20 B.F.A.
SRA/10	Pte. A. Howard	Enteric.	9-7-16	Amara.	...
10488	L/Cpl. D. Ramsay	Dysenter	2-5-16	3 B.G.H.	...
S/10527	Pte. H. Roberts	Enteric.	14-7-16	Amara.	...
1757	Pte. P. Cameron	Drowned	15-8-16	Basrah.	...
S/5414	Pte. R. Craigie	Enteric.	8-7-16	Amara.	...
S/10591	Pte. T. Surgener	Malaria.	15-7-16	Makina.	...
S/10599	Pte. J. Lewis	Enteric.	8-8-16	Sheikh-Saad.	Sheikh-Saad Cemetery, Grave No. 184.
S/11537	Pte. J. Preston	Dysenter	12-10-16	3 B.G.H.	...
S/11540	Pte. W. Mills	Enteric.	14-7-16	Amara.	...
S/11709	Pte. B. McMeechan	Disease.	27-6-16	Sheikh-Saad.	...
S/12115	Pte. A. Robertson	Enteric.	18-7-16	Amara.	...
S/12328	Pte. J. Broadbent	Heat stroke.	5-7-16	"	...
S/12433	Pte. J. Kirkland	Enteric.	24-7-16	"	...
S/12437	Pte. R. Younghusband	"	5-7-16	"	...
S/12474	Pte. J. Porter	Disease.	14-7-16	"	...
S/12519	Pte. J. Christie	Bronche. Pneumor	10-6-16	Alexandria.	...
S/12531	Pte. W. Morrison	Dysenter	22-9-16	Falaheyeh.	...
S/13131	L/Cpl. W. Forbes	"	20-7-16	Basrah.	...
S/13137	Pte. F. Docherty	P.U.O.	28-6-16	Sheikh-Saad.	Sheikh-Saad Cemetery.
S/13144	Pte. S. Lennox	Enteritis.	22-7-16	Basrah.	...
S/13145	Pte. J. McHugh	Typhoid.	28-6-16	Sheikh-Sand.	...
S/13148	Pte. A. McDougall	Enteric.	28-6-16	Amara.	...
S/13154	Pte. E. Ross	Dysenter	20-7-16	"	...
S/13160	L/Cpl. J. Selkirk	Disease.	29-6-16	S.S. Mejidieh.	Christian Burial-ground, Kurna, Row B, Grave 14.
S/13176	Pte. F. Tait	Drowned	23-6-16	Sheikh-Saad.	...
13191	Pte. J. Carroll	Disease.	29-6-16	S.S. Mejidieh.	Christian Burial-ground, Kurna, Row B, Grave 13.

S/13192 Pte. J. Connelly	Heat-stroke.	26-6-16	Sheikh-Saad.	Sheikh-Saad Cemetery.
S/13225 Pte. T. Davidson	Enteric.	2-7-16	Amara.	...
S/13227 Pte. R. Boyd	Enteritis.	30-6-16	The Field.	...
S/13233 Pte. J. Reddie	Heat-stroke.	2-7-16	3 B.G.H.	...
S/13234 Pte. N. Sweeney	Dysenter	21-7-16	Sheikh-Saad.	Sheikh-Saad Cemetery, Grave No. 18.
S/13243 Pte. J. Bain	Disease.	28-6-16	"	" " "
S/13913 Pte. C. McMillan	Malaria.	3-7-16	Amara.	...
S/13982 Pte. J. Duff	Enteric.	8-7-16	"	...
S/13989 Pte. J. King	"	4-3-17	3 B.G.H.	Hakameyeh Cemetery, Grave No. D-9.
S/14009 Pte. G. Carson	Drowned	13-1-17	The Field.	...
S/14016 Pte. A. Flynn	Enteric.	12-7-16	Amara.	...
S/15105 Pte. E. Gay	Dysenter	26-12-16	R. Boat P-53.	...
S/15666 Pte. A. Bewick	Jaundice.	25-6-17	16 C.C. Station.	...
17512 Pte. C. Rattray	Dysenter	7-12-16	32 B.G.H.	Amara Cemetery, Plot C, Row 4, No. 9.

Nominal roll of W.Os., N.C.Os., and men, 2nd Bn., reported 'Missing' or 'Wounded and Missing' during the service of that Unit in I.E.F. "D".

(up to 31st July 1917).

Regimen No.	Rank and Name.	Coy.	
S/7159	L/C. Beattie, L.	4	Missing, 7-1-16.
3/5192	Pte. Black, W.	3	W. and M., 7-1-16.
S/5198	Pte. Dixon, J.	2	Do.
S/10496	L/C. Haig, W.	1	Do.
3/2483	Pte. Hutchison, G.	3	Do.
9661	Pte. McConville, T.	4	Do.
S/7753	Pte. Menelaws, G.	1	Missing, 7-1-16.
S/10323	Pte. Miller, J.	3	W. and M., 7-1-16.
S/8005	Pte. Nicholson, T.	2	Missing, 7-1-16.
3/2901	Pte. Smith, C.	1	Do.
S/7159	Pte. Wilson, G.	4	Do.
S/7056	L/C. Carmichael, B.	1	Missing, 8-1-16.
8408	C.Q.M.S. Jessop, A.	2	Do.
2718	Pte. McKnight, J.	2	Do.
1110	Pte. Duncan, D.	2	Do. Died a Prisoner of War at Mosul, 1-3-16.
S/8257	Pte. Campbell, H.	2	W. and M., 13-1-16.
1891	Pte. Kerwin, J.	1	Missing, 13-1-16.
S/8730	Pte. Rodger, A.	2	W. and M., 13-1-16.
S/8319	Pte. Armstrong, G.	3	W. and M., 21-1-16.
3/3389	Pte. Bain, J.	2	Missing, 21-1-16.
S/9034	Pte. Barnes, C.	1	Do.
1166	Pte. Baxter, F.	1	Do.
1862	L/C. Birse, A.	3	W. and M., 21-1-16.

1891	Pte. Kerwin, J.	1	Missing, 13-1-16.
S/8730	Pte. Rodger, A.	2	W. and M., 13-1-16.
S/8319	Pte. Armstrong, G.	3	W. and M., 21-1-16.
3/3389	Pte. Bain, J.	2	Missing, 21-1-16.
S/9034	Pte. Barnes, C.	1	Do.
1166	Pte. Baxter, F.	1	Do.
1862	L/C. Birse, A.	3	W. and M., 21-1-16.
S/8750	Pte. Bradie, J.	2	Missing, 21-1-16.
S/8496	Pte. Cairns, W.	2	Do.
S/8912	Pte. Chapman, A.	4	Do.
S/8417	Pte. Crerar, J.	2	Do.
S/7104	Pte. Dalziell, G.	2	Do.
1234	Pte. Docherty, N.	1	Do.
3/2872	Pte. Dunleavy, A.	2	Do.
S/8874	Pte. Fairfull, J.	1	Do.
166	A/C. Gair, M.	1	Do.
3/2282	Pte. Garland, P.	4	Do.
10475	Pte. Grey, J.	1	Do.
S/8452	Pte. Hamilton, D.	1	Do.
9260	Sgt. Humm, T.	2	W. and M., 21-1-16.
10338	Pte. Ireland, G.	3	Missing, 21-1-16.
S/10161	Pte. James, G.	4	W. and M., 21-1-16.
S/10147	Pte. Law, S.	1	Missing, 21-1-16.
S/10337	Pte. Leach, R.	1	Do.
1084	Pte. McBride. G.	1	Do.
S/3984	Pte. McComb, A.	1	Do.
SRA/10	Pte. McKenzie, J.	4	Do.
S/7574	Pte. Matheson, P.	1	Do.
S/2941	L/C. Menzies, J.	4	Do.
S/7936	Pte. Mitchell, J.	1	Do.
S/8688	Pte. Mitchell, W.	3	Do.
1921	A/C. Murray, R.	1	Do.
S/10207	A/S. Newton, R.	3	W. and M., 21-1-16.
S/8494	Pte. Ormiston, T.	3	Do.
887	C.S.M. Oswald, W.	1	Missing, 21-1-16.
1802	Pte. Paton, J.	1	Do.
10501	Pte. Pollock, D.	1	Do.
S/7120	Pte. Rennie, S.	2	Do.
659	Pte. Robertson, N.	1	Do.
1605	A/C. Shand, D.	2	Do.
634	Pte. Shaw, J.	3	W. and M., 21-1-16.
3/3970	Pte. Sim, D.	1	Missing, 21-1-16.
S/7658	L/C. Spriggs, W.	3	W. and M., 21-1-16.
8/3854	L/C. Swan, T.	4	Missing, 21-1-16.
S/8880	Pte. Thomson, P.	3	Do.
S/7621	Pte. Vanbeick, A.	2	Do.
S/8744	Pte. Weatherspoon, R.	2	Do.
10242	Pte. Westrop, W.	1	Do.
S/8932	Pte. Whyte D.	3	W. and M., 21-1-16.
S/6733	Pte. Wilkins, E.	1	Missing. 21-1-16.
1989	Pte. Wilson, R.	3	Do.
S/7902	Pte. Worthington, H.	1	W. and M., 21-1-16.
S/10029	Pte. Irving, R.	1	Missing, 28-1-16.

S/7032	Cpl. Cumming, G.	3	W. and M., 6-4-16.
S/10576	Pte. Barbour, W.	2	Missing, 22-4-16.
8/11800	Pte. Beattie, G.	3	Do.
898	Pte. Beveridge, J.	2	Do.
S/10641	Pte. Buchan, J.	2	Do.
S/10579	Pte. Campbell, J.	3	Do.
682	Pte. Carr, A.	4	Do.
S/9850	Pte. Churchard, R.	3	W. and M., 22-4-16.
S/10563	Pte. Clark, T.	2	Missing, 22-4-16.
S/4235	Pte. Cranson, J.	1	Missing, 22-4-16.
S/9562	Pte. Currie, W.	2	Do.
S/8638	Pte. Fleming, W.	2	Missing, 22-4-16. Officially reported killed in action, 22/4.
S/10581	Pte. Ford, W.	3	Missing, 22-4-16.
S/10560	Pte. Gouge, F.	2	Do.
3/8960	Cpl. Green, H.	2	Do.
S/8594	Pte. Hamilton, J.	3	Do.
S/10671	Pte. Hamilton, D.	2	Do.
S/10644	Pte. Henderson, W.	4	W. and M., 22-4-16.
S/11758	Pte. Kirkham, W.	2	Missing, 22-4-16.
S/9501	Pte. Lauchlan, W.	2	Do.
S/10568	Pte. Low, W.	2	Do.
S/11966	Pte. McCarthy, A.	2	Do.
S/10135	Pte. McGlennon, J.	2	Do.
3/4223	Pte. McGregor, A.	4	Do.
S/10662	Pte. McLaren, J.	2	Do.
1889	Pte. McLean, R.	3	Do.
2635	Pte. Marshall, D.	1	Do.
S/4379	Pte. Marshall, G.	3	Do.
S/7697	Pte. Montgomery, H.	1	Do.
S/11286	Pte. Morgan, G.	4	W. and M., 22-4-16.
S/3346	Pte. Morrison, D.	1	Missing, 22-4-16.
8166	Pte. Morrison, S.	1	Do.
S/10536	L/C. Ramsay, J.	2	Do.
S/11751	Pte. Russell, J.	2	Do.
S/11557	Pte. Smith, A.	2	Do.
S/11753	Pte. Smith, E.	2	Do.
S/3708	Pte. Sinclair, J.	1	Do.
S/11390	Pte. Stewart, J.	1	Do.
S/11607	Pte. Styles, S.	1	Do.
1459	L/C. Torrance, G.	3	Do.
S/4076	Pte. Walker, J.	1	W. and M., 22-4-16.
7908	C.S.M. Wilkie, A.	1	Missing, 22-4-16.
2772	Pte. Whyte, R.	4	Missing, 22-4-16. Officially accepted as having died between 22-4-16 and 2-2-17.
S/4239	Pte. Wilson, R.	1	Missing, 22-4-16.
S/10674	Pte. Wilson, J.	2	Missing, 22-4-17. Officially reported killed in action, 22-4-16.
S/10668	Pte. Wilson, J.	2	Missing, 22-4-16.
S/10540	L/C. Wood, C.	1	Missing, 22-4-16. Officially reported killed in action, 22-4-16.
S/15657	Pte. Carlyle, W.	1	Missing, 14-3-17.

15613	Pte. Cook, J.	1	W. and M. 14-3-17.
3/10222	Pte. Harris, A.	2	Do.
S/11776	Pte. Hewitt, G.	1	Do.
S/11307	L/C. Hutchison, J.	1	Do.
S/15892	Pte. Jennings, R.	1	Do.
S/15080	Pte. Watt, J.	4	Do.
S/13905	Pte. Batchelor, C.	3	Missing, 21-4-17.
S/11835	Pte. Burnett, W.	3	Do.
S/3569	Pte. Campbell, J.	4	Do.
17494	Pte. Gilfillan, T.	2	Do.

TOTAL   125   Of whom 4 have now been officially reported as died or killed in action.

Total Missing, battle of 7th Jan. 1916		11
Do.	do. 13th January 1916	3
Do.	do. 21st January 1916	50
Do.	do. 22nd April 1916	44
Do.	do. 14th March 1917	7
Do.	do. 21st April 1917	4
Missing, various dates		6

PRISONERS OF WAR.

Regimen No.	Rank and Name	Coy.	
SRA/10	Pte. Cottle, T.	1	Pris. of War, Mosul. Captured, 7-1-16.
S/11543	Pte. McDonald, G.	..	Pris. of War, Afion Kara Hissar, Captured 22-4-16.
SRA/10	Pte. Debnam, J.	4	Captured, 21-1-16. Released in September 1916 and invalided to India.

After a period of severe and strenuous fighting extending with only short pauses over a period of two months, I wish to express to the Navy, to Lieutenant-Generals Marshall and Cobb, to the Divisional and Brigade Commanders, to the staffs including my own and to all ranks of the fighting troops, my warmest thanks for their splendid work and my congratulations on their brilliant successes. To the Regimental Officers, N.C.Os. and men, a special word is due for their matchless heroism and fighting spirit, and for their grit and determination so fully in accord with the best traditions of British and Indian Regiments.

Whilst regretting deeply the casualties necessarily incurred in the attainment of our object, the series of stinging blows dealt to the enemy, his severe losses which are out of all proportion to the size of his force and his obviously faltering spirit afford ample proof to all ranks that their sacrifices have not been made in vain. My thanks too are due to Major-General MacMunn, to the Director and their assistants and to all ranks of the Administrative Services and Departments, both in the field and on the lines of communication who in face of unexampled difficulties have by sterling work and energy risen superior to them and regularly met the needs of the fighting troops with ample supplies, stores and munitions without which the loss of lives would have been considerably increased and success rendered impossible, and have been the means of providing every comfort, attainable for the sick and wounded.

To each and every member of the Navy and Army and to those who, though not belonging to either of the services have helped to bring about the results achieved I tender my earnest thanks for their wholehearted and magnificent efforts. The end is not yet; but with such absolute co-operation and vigour animating all continuance of our success is assured.

(SD.) F. S. Maude, Lieut.-Gent.,

Commanding I.E.F. "D."

15th February 1917.

I have received the following message from His Imperial Majesty the King-Emperor:—

March 11th.—It is with greatest satisfaction that I have received the good news that you have occupied Baghdad. I heartily congratulate you and your troops on the success achieved under so many difficulties.—George R.I.

I have sent the following reply:—

March 12th.—Your Imperial Majesty's gracious message has been communicated to all ranks of the forces serving in Mesopotamia by whom it has been received with feelings of intense gratitude, loyalty and devotion. The difficulties by which we have been confronted have only increased our determination to surmount them.

The following are some of the other messages received and replies sent:—

From His Excellency the Viceroy of India:—
March 13th.—My most hearty congratulations to yourself and the troops under your command on the capture of Baghdad which has been achieved by their gallantry and devotion to duty.

March 14th.—Your Excellency's kind message has been received with sincere gratitude by all ranks of the forces in Mesopotamia. Nothing could have exceeded the valour and endurance of the troops both British and Indian under trying conditions.

From The Grand Duke Nicholas:—
March 10th.—I and the Caucasus Army send heartiest congratulations on the new success won by the glorious troops under your command. The Caucasus Army will do all in their power to further your developments and successes.

March 12th.—On behalf of the troops serving in Mesopotamia I beg to thank your Imperial Highness very warmly for kind message which is much appreciated by us all. Our Russian comrades in Caucasus may rest assured that we shall continue to do our utmost to assist their operations already so successfully commenced.

From the Right Hon'ble the Secretary of State for War:—
March 13th.—His Majesty's Government desire me to convey to you and all ranks under your command their cordial congratulations on the noble feat of arms which has led to your occupation of Baghdad. They fully recognise the difficulties which you have faced and overcome and wish to express their high appreciation of the skilful plan of operations, the careful co-ordination of the administrative work and the courage and endurance of the troops.

March 14th.—Your message conveying approbation of His Majesty's Government with respect to our efforts has been received with widespread pleasure by all ranks of the forces in Mesopotamia. The difficulties by which we were met were soon swept aside by the dauntless valour and endurance of the troops ably seconded by the thorough and smooth working of the administrative services.

From His Excellency the Commander-in-Chief in India:—
March 12th.—To you and your gallant troops I desire to convey my own and the warmest congratulations of all ranks in India on your splendid achievements. The valour, devotion to duty and determination which have defeated a stubborn enemy and culminated in the capture of Baghdad evoke our highest admiration."

March 14th.—All ranks of the forces in Mesopotamia thank Your Excellency most warmly for your most kind message. It is a particular source of satisfaction to us to feel that our efforts are appreciated so thoroughly by our comrades in India. British and Indian troops have vied with each other in valour and endurance and difficulties met with have only stimulated our determination to surmount them.

From Admiral Sir David Beatty, G.C.B., K.C.V.O., D.S.O.:—
March 12th.—Please accept, on behalf of the Grand Fleet and myself, our admiration and congratulations upon the magnificent achievement in capturing Baghdad by the gallant forces under your command."

March 14th.—Your message has been received with widespread pleasure by all ranks of the forces in Mesopotamia. During operations the Navy has, as usual, played its part nobly. We are particularly proud at receiving congratulations from the Grand Fleet, which has itself done much superb work consistently during past two and a half years.

From Field Marshal Sir Douglas Haig, G.C.B., G.C.V.O., K.C.I.E., Commander-in-Chief Armies in France:—

March 16th.—Your brilliant achievements and continued successes are a great delight and a great encouragement to all ranks under my command."

March 16th.—Most grateful for kind message—much valued."

From Vice-Admiral Sir Rosslyn E. Wemyss, K.C.B., C.M.G., M.V.O., Naval Commander-in-Chief, British East Indies:—

March 14th.—Please accept hearty congratulations of self and whole of Indian Squadron on your splendid success. I am proud to think that the Royal Navy has been able to co-operate with your troops."

March 16th.—Most grateful to you and East Indies Squadron for kind message. Royal Navy here have co-operated with our operations brilliantly."

From General Sir Archibald Murray, K.C.B., K.C.M.G., C.V.O., D.S.O., Commander-in-Chief, Egyptian Expeditionary force:—

Your splendid series of successes are being watched with the profoundest delight and gratification by all ranks of the Egyptian Force. Bridging operations must have been grandly carried out. Once more our heartiest congratulations.

Most grateful for kind message. All ranks appreciate it, especially coming as it does from a Commander and troops who have themselves done so brilliantly. Our troops here have been quite magnificent.

From Lieut.-General G. F. Milne, C.B., D.S.O., Commander-in-Chief British Forces at Salonika:—

March 12th.—Hearty congratulations to you and your Army from all ranks of the Salonika Force.

March 13th.—We all thank you very warmly for kind message.

From Major-General A. R. Hoskins, C.M.G., D.S.O., Commanding East African Force:—

March 13th.—Hearty congratulations from all ranks East African Force to Mesopotamian Force on brilliant achievements."

March 16th.—Most grateful for kind message much appreciated by us all.

From the Right Hon'ble the Lord Mayor of London:—
March 13th.—The City of London sends hearty congratulations on the capture of the historic City of Baghdad."

March 14th.—Your Lordship's kind message conveying congratulations of the City of London is very warmly appreciated by all ranks of the forces in Mesopotamia. Qualities of courage and endurance displayed by troops throughout operations have been superb."

F. S. Maude, Lieut.-General,
Commanding Indian Expeditionary Force "D."
30th March 1917.

GENERAL HEAD QUARTERS.
I.E.F. "D."
ORDER OF THE DAY, No. 66.

In pursuance of the authority delegated to me by His Imperial Majesty the King-Emperor, I make the following awards for gallantry and distinguished service in the field:—

Awarded the Military Cross.

Captain Robert Macfarlane—For conspicuous gallantry and devotion to duty. Although wounded early in the action he continued to lead his Company with great determination until the evening, when the position was finally taken by a bayonet charge. With great courage and skill he led his Company up to a position from which he was able to enfilade the enemy at close range, thereby greatly assisting the charge.

Second-Lieutenant Benjamin Smith Houston,—For conspicuous gallantry and ability in leading the second line of his battalion with excellent judgment under heavy fire. After reinforcing the first line he took command of the left portion of it including some 60 men of an Indian Infantry regiment who were without an officer and led them on during the charge and subsequent advance on the railway station. He had recently done fine work when in command of a patrol.

Awarded the Distinguished Conduct Medal.

No. 1081, Sergeant James Strachan—For conspicuous gallantry and ability in action. When all four of his Company Officers had been wounded, he took command of the left flank of the battalion. He ably directed their fire and later led forward what remained of his company across the open and drove the enemy out of his position taking some prisoners.

No. 19438, Lance-Corporal George Mcgabe,—For conspicuous gallantry and resource during operations. Seeing that a gap existed between an Indian Regiment and his own, and that the former in this locality had lost all their officers, he took charge of their Lewis guns and filled the gap. Later, he was conspicuous for his gallantry in leading the Indian Infantrymen in the charge across the open.

Awarded the Military Medal.

No. 2262, Sergeant Frank Connel.

F. S. Maude, Lieut.-General,
Commanding I.E.F. "D".

31st March 1917.

GENERAL HEAD QUARTERS.
I.E.F. "D."
ORDER OF THE DAY, No. 76.

His Imperial Majesty the King-Emperor, has conveyed the following message to me:—

May 8th.—The series of successes achieved in defeating the Turkish Forces brought against you since your capture of Baghdad reflect the very highest credit upon you and all ranks under your command. Your progress is all the more appreciated by your fellow countrymen in that they are conscious of the trying conditions under which your troops have fought.—George R.I.

The following reply has been sent by me:—

May 9th.—Your Imperial Majesty's gracious message expressing approbation of our recent successes has filled all ranks of the Navy and Army in Mesopotamia with loyal enthusiasm. The valour and devotion to duty of the troops conscious of their superiority over the enemy have been superb, whilst in spite of great heat recently experienced their health remains most satisfactory.

From the Right Hon'ble the Secretary of State for War:—
May 8th.—War Cabinet desire me to convey their high appre-

ciation of your recent operations which have resulted in the defeat of the enemy's forces and the successful occupation of the greater part of the Baghdad Vilayat. The splendid spirit and gallantry displayed by the troops under trying climatic conditions and the skill shown by your subordinate commanders merit high commendation and are a proof of the efficiency and devotion to duty of all ranks of the force under your command.

May 9th.—Your telegram conveying approval of War Cabinet at success of our recent operations is greatly appreciated by all ranks in Mesopotamia. Fighting spirit and endurance of troops have been admirable throughout in spite of great heat recently.

F. S. Maude, Lieut.-General,
Commanding Indian Expeditionary Force "D."

11th May 1917.

GENERAL HEAD QUARTERS.
I.E.F. "D."
ORDER OF THE DAY, NO. 82.

In pursuance of the authority delegated to me by His Imperial Majesty the King-Emperor, I make the following award for gallantry and distinguished service in the field:—

Awarded a Bar to Distinguished Conduct Medal.

No. 1543, Sergeant Charles Easton.—For conspicuous gallantry in action. Seeing that an officer had been hit some 80 yards in front of his post and was unable to move owing to continuous sniping, he ran forward, dressed his wounds, and got him back to the river bank. As sniping still continued, he swam the river, supporting the wounded Officer, and gained the other bank. Had the Officer not been moved, he must again have been hit by the enemy's snipers who were within 300 yards.

F. S. Maude, Lieut.-General,
Commanding Indian Expeditionary Force "D."

17th June 1917.

GENERAL HEAD QUARTERS.
MESOPOTAMIAN EXPEDITIONARY FORCE.
ORDER OF THE DAY, NO. 96.

In pursuance of the authority delegated to me by His Imperial Majesty the King-Emperor, I make the following awards for gallantry and distinguished service in connection with operations in the field covering the period April 1st to September 30th, 1917, inclusive.

Awarded Second Bar to Distinguished Conduct Medal.

No. 2702, Sergeant William Logan.—For conspicuous gallantry and ability. At a critical moment he led forward a party of bombers under heavy fire and controlled them with great skill until wounded. By his courage and coolness he materially assisted in repelling a counter-attack and in retaking a redoubt, [Awarded D.C.M., *London Gazette*, 20th October, 1916, Bar to D.C.M., *London Gazette*, 29th August, 1917].

Awarded the Distinguished Conduct Medal.

No. 3-2377, Private George Beveridge.—For conspicuous gallantry and initiative. He repeatedly carried messages back from the firing line under heavy fire and, at a critical moment, rallied his comrades after a counter-attack and led them to the final capture of the position. His courage and dash were most marked.

No. 2334, Private Joseph Clark.—For conspicuous gallantry and devotion to duty. He displayed great resource and initiative in re-organising both British and Indian troops after a counter-attack, in time to meet successfully a second one. His bravery and coolness throughout the day greatly encouraged his men. He has done fine work on other occasions.

GENERAL HEAD QUARTERS.

MESOPOTAMIAN EXPEDITIONARY FORCE.

ORDER OF THE DAY. NO. 102.

The following extract from the *London Gazette* is published for general information:—

His Majesty the King has been graciously pleased to approve of the award of the Victoria Cross to the undermentioned Officers, Non-commissioned Officers and Men:—

War Office,
26th November 1917.

No. 871, Private Charles Melvin, Highlander Regiment (*Kirriemuir*).—For most conspicuous bravery, coolness and resource in action. Pte. Melvin's Company had advanced to within fifty yards of the front-line trench of a redoubt, where, owing to the intensity of the enemy's fire, the men were obliged to lie down and wait for reinforcements. Pte. Melvin, however, rushed on by himself, over ground swept from end to end by rifle and machine gun fire. On reaching the enemy trench, he halted and fired two or three shots into it, killing one or two enemy, but as the others in the trench continued to fire at him, he jumped into it, and attacked them with his bayonet in his hand, as owing to his rifle being damaged, it was not "fixed."

On being attacked in this resolute manner most of the enemy fled to their second line, but not before Pte. Melvin had killed two more and succeeded in disarming eight unwounded and one wounded. Pte. Melvin bound up the wounds of the wounded man, and then driving his eight unwounded prisoners before him, and supporting the wounded one he hustled them out of the trench, marched them in and delivered them over to an officer.

He then provided himself with a load of ammunition and returned to the firing line where he reported himself to his platoon sergeant. All this was done, not only under intense rifle and machine gun fire, but the whole way back Pte. Melvin and his party were exposed to a very heavy artillery barrage fire. Throughout the day Pte. Melvin greatly inspired those near him with confidence and courage.

W. R. Marshall, Lieut.-General,

Commanding-in-Chief,

Mesopotamian Expeditionary Force.

General Headquarters,
6th March 1918.

LEONAUR

ALSO FROM LEONAUR
AVAILABLE IN SOFTCOVER OR HARDCOVER WITH DUST JACKET

A HISTORY OF THE FRENCH & INDIAN WAR *by Arthur G. Bradley*—The Seven Years War as it was fought in the New World has always fascinated students of military history—here is the story of that confrontation.

WASHINGTON'S EARLY CAMPAIGNS *by James Hadden*—The French Post Expedition, Great Meadows and Braddock's Defeat—including Braddock's Orderly Books.

BOUQUET & THE OHIO INDIAN WAR *by Cyrus Cort & William Smith*—Two Accounts of the Campaigns of 1763-1764: Bouquet's Campaigns by Cyrus Cort & The History of Bouquet's Expeditions by William Smith.

NARRATIVES OF THE FRENCH & INDIAN WAR: 2 *by David Holden, Samuel Jenks, Lemuel Lyon, Mary Cochrane Rogers & Henry T. Blake*—Contains The Diary of Sergeant David Holden, Captain Samuel Jenks' Journal, The Journal of Lemuel Lyon, Journal of a French Officer at the Siege of Quebec, A Battle Fought on Snowshoes & The Battle of Lake George.

NARRATIVES OF THE FRENCH & INDIAN WAR *by Brown, Eastburn, Hawks & Putnam*—Ranger Brown's Narrative, The Adventures of Robert Eastburn, The Journal of Rufus Putnam—Provincial Infantry & Orderly Book and Journal of Major John Hawks on the Ticonderoga-Crown Point Campaign.

THE 7TH (QUEEN'S OWN) HUSSARS: Volume 1—1688-1792 *by C. R. B. Barrett*—As Dragoons During the Flanders Campaign, War of the Austrian Succession and the Seven Years War.

INDIA'S FREE LANCES *by H. G. Keene*—European Mercenary Commanders in Hindustan 1770-1820.

THE BENGAL EUROPEAN REGIMENT *by P. R. Innes*—An Elite Regiment of the Honourable East India Company 1756-1858.

MUSKET & TOMAHAWK *by Francis Parkman*—A Military History of the French & Indian War, 1753-1760.

THE BLACK WATCH AT TICONDEROGA *by Frederick B. Richards*—Campaigns in the French & Indian War.

QUEEN'S RANGERS *by Frederick B. Richards*—John Simcoe and his Rangers During the Revolutionary War for America.